T0135765

The influence of a self-avatar on space and body perception in immersive virtual reality

Dissertation

der Mathematisch-Naturwissenschaftlichen Fakultät

der Eberhard Karls Universität Tübingen

zur Erlangung des Grades eines

Doktors der Naturwissenschaften

(Dr. rer. nat.)

vorgelegt von

Ivelina Vesselinova Piryankova

aus Kyustendil/Bulgarien

Tübingen

2014

Bibliografische Information der Deutschen Nationalbibliothek

Die Deutsche Nationalbibliothek verzeichnet diese Publikation in der
Deutschen Nationalbibliografie; detaillierte bibliografische Daten sind
im Internet über http://dnb.d-nb.de abrufbar.

ISBN 978-3-8325-3978-8

Logos Verlag Berlin GmbH
Comeniushof, Gubener Str. 47,
10243 Berlin
Tel.: +49 (0)30 42 85 10 90
Fax: +49 (0)30 42 85 10 92
INTERNET: http://www.logos-verlag.de

Gedruckt mit Genehmigung der Mathematisch-Naturwissenschaftlichen Fakultät der Eberhard Karls Universität Tübingen.

Tag der mündlichen Qualifikation:	26.02.2015
Dekan:	Prof. Dr. Wolfgang Rosenstiel
1. Berichterstatter:	Prof. Dr. Andreas Schilling
2. Berichterstatter:	Dr. Betty J. Mohler

"A person starts to live
when he can live outside himself."
Albert Einstein [1]

This PhD thesis is dedicated to my family,
for their endless love and support.

ABSTRACT

The technological advances in computer graphics, three-dimensional scanning and motion tracking technologies, contribute to the increase in the use of self-avatars in immersive real time virtual reality (VR) for visualization, simulation, clinical VR and entertainment purposes. Therefore, it is important to gain new insights on how users perceive their body, their self-avatar and the virtual space, as well as the interaction between body and space perception in VR. Using state-of-the-art VR technologies, I investigated how changes of the self-avatar influence the perception of one's own body and space in VR. I demonstrate that self-avatars do not need to have the exact same size as the user's physical body in order for the user's to identify with their self-avatar. After providing specific sensory information the users can adapt to a self-avatar, even if the avatar has a considerably different size. In addition, the user's perception of actions in the virtual space can be biased by the size of their stylized self-avatar. Further, I conducted several experiments in large screen immersive displays (LSIDs) to determine the optimal position of the personalized self-avatars when veridical body and space perception in VR is desired. I found that distances in the tested LSIDs are underestimated (compared to nearly veridical perception in the real world). Additionally, the accuracy of the distance judgments depended on the indicated distance in the distance judgment task. Considering these findings, I designed an experiment in which I investigated women's sensitivity to changes in their perceived weight. The body mass index of the participants' personalized avatars was altered and the availability of visual cues like texture and shape of the personalized avatar were manipulated. I found that weight was perceived veridically regardless of body shape (average female shape or own shape generated from three-dimensional scanning data). Interestingly, the texture of the self-avatar influenced the perception of body weight. Avatars with a checkerboard texture appeared to be significantly bigger as compared to those with a photorealistic texture. I also found that there is a range within which the weight of the personalized self-avatar is perceived to be the same as the user's weight. For women this range is shifted towards their ideal weight. This research has major implications for improving the usefulness of clinical VR (e.g. therapies and diagnostics), specifically, for gaining new insights on the body perception of individuals with body image distortions (i.e. stroke and eating disorder patients). These results are also useful for researchers and developers interested in designing VR applications (e.g. games, visualization and entertainment) that use self-avatars and aim at providing a realistic experience in VR.

ZUSAMMENFASSUNG

Technologische Fortschritte in der Computergrafik, dem dreidimensionalen Scannen und in Motion-Tracking-Technologien haben zu einem erhöhten Einsatz von Selbst-Avataren in immersiven virtuellen Realitäten (VR) beigetragen. Selbst-Avatare werden zum Beispiel in den Bereichen Visualisierung und Simulation, aber auch in klinischen Anwendungen oder für Unterhaltungszwecke eingesetzt. Deshalb ist es wichtig neue Erkenntnisse über die Wahrnehmung des eigenen Körpers, des Selbst-Avatars und der räumlichen Wahrnehmung des Benutzers zu gewinnen, sowie den Einfluss des Selbst-Avatars auf die räumliche Wahrnehmung in der virtuellen Welt zu untersuchen. Mit Hilfe von moderner VR-Technologie habe ich untersucht wie Veränderungen des Selbst-Avatars die Wahrnehmung des eigenen Körpers und des Raumes verändern. Die Ergebnisse zeigen, dass Selbst-Avatare nicht genau die gleichen Dimensionen wie der Körper des Benutzers haben müssen, damit sich der Benutzer mit seinem Selbst-Avatar identifizieren kann. Wenn die virtuelle Welt dem Benutzer bestimmte sensorische Informationen bereitstellt, können sich die Benutzer mit ihrem Selbst-Avatar auch dann identifizieren, auch wenn der Avatar deutlich andere Dimensionen als der physikalische Körper des Benutzers aufweist. Zudem kann die Wahrnehmung von Aktionen in der virtuellen Umgebung durch die Körpergröße des Selbst-Avatars beeinflusst werden. Weiterhin wurden mehrere Experimente mit großen immersiven Bildschirmen durchgeführt, um die optimale Positionierung eines personalisierten Selbst-Avatars in der virtuellen Umgebung zu bestimmen. Dadurch kann eine möglichst wahrheitsgetreue Wahrnehmung des Avatars und der umgebenden virtuellen Welt erreicht werden. Die Ergebnisse zeigen, dass im Vergleich zu einer fast wahrheitsgetreuen Distanzwahrnehmung in der realen Welt, Entfernungen in großen immersiven Bildschirmen unterschätzt werden. Zusätzlich hängt die Genauigkeit der Abstandsschätzungen in virtuellen Umgebungen auch von der zu schätzenden Distanz ab. Unter Berücksichtigung dieser Ergebnisse habe ich ein Experiment entwickelt, um die Sensitivität der Gewichtswahrnehmung von Frauen bezüglich Veränderungen ihres Körpergewichts zu untersuchen. Der Body-Mass-Index der personalisierten Avatare der Probandinnen wurde systematisch verändert und die Verfügbarkeit der visuellen Merkmale wie Textur und Form der Avatare wurde manipuliert. Die Ergebnisse zeigen, dass die Probandinnen ihr Gewicht sehr genau einschätzen können und zwar unabhängig von der Körperform (durchschnittliche weibliche Form oder eigene Form basierend auf dreidimensionalen Scandaten der Probandinnen). Interessanterweise, hat die Textur des Selbst-Avatars die Einschätzung des Körpergewichts beeinflusst. Avatare mit einer einfachen Schachbrettmustertextur erschienen deutlich schwerer hinsichtlich des Körpergewichts als Avatare mit fotorealistischen Texturen. Außerdem hat sich gezeigt, dass es einen Bereich gibt in dem das Gewicht des personalisierten Selbst-Avatars noch als dasselbe wie das Eigene von den Probandinnen eingeschätzt wird. Dieser Bereich ist hin zum Idealgewicht der Probandinnen verschoben. Die Ergebnisse dieser Forschung können zur Verbesserung von VR Anwendungen im klinischen Bereich beitragen (z.B. Therapien und Diagnostika), da die in dieser Dissertation demonstrierten und getesteten Methoden auch genutzt werden können, um neue Erkenntnisse über die Körperwahrnehmung von Menschen mit zum Beispiel Schlaganfällen oder Essstörungen zu gewinnen. Zudem können die präsentierten Ergebnisse von Forschern und Entwicklern von VR Anwendungen (z.B. Spiele, Visualisierungsanwendungen, Animationsanwendungen) genutzt werden, um eine realistische Erfahrung in virtuellen Welten und dazu passende Selbst-Avatare zu schaffen.

ACKNOWLEDGMENTS

First and foremost, I would like to express my gratefulness to my supervisor from Max Planck Institute for Biological Cybernetics Dr. Betty Mohler for her support, constructive criticism and friendly advices. I would like to thank my supervisor from Eberhard Karls University, Tübingen Prof. Dr. Andreas Schilling for useful discussions and feedback regarding my research. I sincerely want to thank Prof. Dr. Heinrich H. Bülthoff for his support not only in my research related to my PhD thesis, but also in other projects. I would like to express my appreciation to my committee members, Dr. Betty Mohler, Prof. Dr. Andreas Schilling, Juniorprof. Dr. Alexandra Kirsch and Prof. Dr. Heinrich H. Bülthoff for their time and interest in my research.

The research projects in which I did during my thesis would have not been possible without the support of the Max Planck Society and the funding from the Center for Integrative Neuroscience, Tuebingen CIN2011-16, as well as the support of the World Class University (WCU) program through the National Research Foundation of Korea funded by the Ministry of Education, Science and Technology (R31-2008-000-10008-0). I am thankful for being involved in a tandem project from the Center for Integrative Neuroscience and having the opportunity to work with fascinating researchers from various backgrounds. I would like to express my appreciation to Dr. Hong Yu Wong, Dr. Catherine Stinson, Dr. Matthew R. Longo and the research group of Prof. Dr. Michael Black, from the Perceiving Systems department at Max Planck Institute for Intelligent Systems, specifically Dr. Javier Romero, Naureen Mahmood, Dr. Eric Rachlin, Jessica Purmort, Emma-Jayne Holderness and Sophie Lupas, for helpful suggestions and insightful discussions.

I am sincerely grateful to Prof. Dr. Jeanine Stefanucci, Dr. Hong Yu Wong and Stephan de la Rosa for sharing their truthful views and providing insightful suggestions for improving my work. I would like to thank to Reuben Fleming and Dr. Martin Breidt for useful discussions related to 3D modeling and graphics. I would like to thank to my colleagues, Dr. Ekaterina Volkova, Aurelie Saulton, Dr. Trevor Dodds, Dr. Markus Leyrer, Dr. Florian Soyka, Dr. Michael Geuss, Dr. Martin Dobricki, Rainer Boss, Anna Wellerdiek, Dr. Stephan Streuber, Dr. Tobias Meilinger and Dr. Sally A. Linkenauger for the enjoyable working environment and for enthusiastic discussions about science. Also, I would like to thank to Joachim Tesch and Michael Kerger for technical support and help with the VR equipment.

Finally, words cannot express my gratefulness to my husband Tancho Piryankov, my brother Martin Alexandrov and my parents Nikolina and Vesselin Alexandrovi for their love and constant support throughout my life and especially over the last three years. At the end I would like to thank my son Daniel Piryankov for making my life full of joy and happiness.

CONTENTS

ACRONYMS

1st PP	First-person Perspective
2AFC	One Interval Forced Choice With Two Response Alternatives
2D	Two-dimensional
3D	Three-dimensional
3rd PP	Third-person Perspective
BMI	Body Mass Index
CoP	Center of Projection
FOV	Field Of View
HMD	Head-mounted Display
IPD	Interpupillary Distance
IVE	Immersive Virtual Environment
LSID	Large Screen Immersive Display
MPI	Max Planck Institute
PSE	Point Of Subjective Equality
RHI	Rubber Hand Illusion
VE	Virtual Environment
VR	Virtual Reality

INTRODUCTION

The technological advances in display, three-dimensional (3D) scanning and motion tracking technologies, as well as the high computation speed, realistic graphics and rendering contribute to the rapid development of low-cost and largely accessible virtual reality (VR) systems and applications. Therefore, VR setups are progressively becoming a preferable medium for applications used for visualization, simulations, training, therapeutic and entertainment purposes [2]. VR is generally used as a medium for simulation of a variety of real world scenarios [3, 4, 5], such as reconstructions of medical scenarios for medical training [6, 7], rehabilitation [8], military trainings [2, 4, 9], as well as design, planning [10, 11] and assembly processes [10, 11]. One reason for this is that VR simulations are less labor-intensive for the trainers and the trainees [4]. Additionally, VR is a safe environment for simulation of processes and training of scenarios involving health threatening tasks, such as emergency and military simulations [9]. Hence, VR enables the exploration of research areas that cannot be tested in a real world setup. Additionally, the virtual worlds used in VR can be manipulated easier than the real world environments. For instance, the size or the material of a virtual object or avatar can be easily changed. Whereas in the real world changing the material of an object or the physical size of a person might not be even possible. Thus, VR provides a controlled environment for investigating space and body perception [4, 12, 13].

VR is often used as a medium for visualization and simulation of a variety of real world scenarios

Ideally, VR should provide experience that makes the user behave in a similar way to their real world behavior. It has been shown that by providing the viewer the illusion of being present in the virtual world, one can enhance realistic responses to events simulated in realistic virtual environments (VEs) [14, 15]. Additionally, the user of the VE simulations should perceive the 3D spatial layout, as the designer of the virtual world intends [16]. For this reason the developers of VR applications try to design realistic virtual worlds by modeling realistic buildings rendered with realistic lighting and materials and populating the virtual worlds using virtual avatars.

VEs should be designed so, that VR evokes the realistic responses of the user

To improve the realism of the virtual worlds and the usefulness of VR technology, scientists have investigated the differences between the real and the virtual world, with respect to the sensory information provided in the virtual world, as well as with regard to the user's perception and action [14, 15, 17]. One major difference has been found in spatial perception [18, 19, 20, 21, 22, 23, 24, 25, 26]. In particular, people veridically estimate egocentric distances in the real world (at least up to about 20m [18]), but underestimate egocentric distances in immersive HMD VEs (even up to 50% [19, 27]) [25, 26, 28, 29, 30]. Egocentric distance is often used for providing information about space perception in both real and virtual worlds. Egocentric distance

Understanding space and body perception is beneficial for the effectiveness of VR applications

The absolute distance between the observer and an external point in space is called egocentric distance

is the absolute distance between the observer and an external point in space
[31].

Generally, in the immersive VEs the users are either not visually represented at all or represented by *virtual avatars*[1] in the VE, more specifically

Self-avatars are human-like stylized or personalized characters

self-avatars. The self-avatars are usually human-like stylized or personalized
characters, which are visualized to the user in first-person perspective (1st PP)
(the self-avatar is collocated with the user's body in the real world) or third-
person perspective (3rd PP) (the self-avatar is not collocated with the user's
body in the real world). In terms of animation self-avatars can be static (e.g.
Chapter 5 [37] and Chapter 7 [38]) or animated with predefined or with the
user's motions (e.g. [39, 40] - 1st PP self-avatar; [6, 7] - 3rd PP self-avatar).
For many VR applications to be effective, people need to identify themselves
with their self-avatar and feel ownership over their virtual body. This is particularly important for clinical VR applications (e.g. therapy or rehabilitation)
that aim at helping or stimulating the patients to perform tasks, which are difficult for them to perform in the real world.

1.1   OUTLINE OF THE THESIS

In this thesis I use immersive VR as a medium to investigate the own body
perception and perception of self-avatar, as well as their influence on the sur-

I investigate the perception of the physical body and the self-avatar, as well as their influence on the surrounding space

rounding virtual space. Considering the topic of the thesis and its implications there are several different research areas related to VR and perception
that are of great importance to this research. Therefore, in the current chapter
I introduce the term VR and its applications, as well as the aim and the novel
contribution of the thesis to computer graphics and perception research in VR.
In Chapter 2, I provide a brief summary of state-of-the-art avatars and immersive display technologies used in current VR setups and applications. Based
on related research outlined in Chapter 3 and the state-of-the-art avatars presented in Chapter 2, I describe the motivation for this research in Chapter
4.

The research of this thesis investigates the conditions required for embodying a virtual avatar and introduces novel measures to assess embodiment of a
virtual avatar (see Chapter 5). Further, in Chapter 6, I explore the impact of
viewing one's physical body on the perception of space in large screen immersive display (LSID) VEs. These findings provide new insights which I use for
designing the VR setup for an experiment in which I investigate women's[2]

---

1 Beyond the scope of this research are two other types of virtual avatars. First, virtual avatars
that are used to simulate a crowd of humans that populate the virtual world, have human-like
motions and talk to each other in small groups, such as the crowd simulations presented in the
work of McDonnell and O'Sullivan 2010 and Ennis et al. 2010. Second, virtual avatars used
to visualize artificial intelligence systems, which are designed to simulate real humans. These
systems are also called *virtual humans*. They can have their own personality, emotional and
human-like behavior, as well as human-like way to communicate and interact with the user
[34, 35, 36].

2 I used only female participants in the experiment presented in Chapters 5 and 7 mainly because
there is a sex difference in the way people perceive the size of their *physical* body (see [41] for
an overview). Since I am manipulating the size of the virtual avatar, the results of the research

sensitivity to changes in their perceived weight by altering the body mass index (BMI) ($BMI = \frac{weight(kg)}{height(m)^2}$) of the participants' personalized avatars displayed on a LSID VE (see Chapter 7). Finally, after discussing the main findings (see chapter 8) and listing the major implications of this thesis (see Chapter 9) which relate to computer graphics, clinical VR, clothing industry and body and space perception research in VR, I summarize this research in Chapter 10.

1.2   VIRTUAL REALITY

The term VR was first associated with the theater and the engagement of the viewer in an illusory and visionary world presented in the theater play through the characters, the objects and the images on the stage [44]:

VR was first associated with the illusory world presented in the theater play

   "...the theater also takes gestures and pushes them as far as they will go: like the plague it reforges the chain between what is and what is not, between the virtuality of the possible and what already exists in materialized nature. ..." [44, p.27]

   However, around 1960 the term VR evolves (from an experience associated with the theater) to describe immersive multimedia systems with computer interfaces, which use a variety of technologies to provide the user with an immersive sensory experience of being in a simulated, virtual space [45, 46, 47, 48, 49]. Inventions, such as *Sensorama* (patented in 1962) and *Rocket ship amusement* [50], as well as envisions, such as *the ultimate display* (described in [49]) put the foundations of the technology currently used for VR systems [5].

Currently VR is related to technologies that provide the user with an immersive sensory experience of being in a simulated space

   The VR systems used nowadays still provide different modalities in order to simulate realistic experiences. In general, the sensory experience provided to the user by the current VR systems is usually by stimulating visual and auditory modalities, but many systems also provide additional sensory feedback such as motion feedback, haptic or olfactory modality (sense of smell). The sensory experience is created through a combination of state-of-the-art technologies, such as immersive displays, motion tracking systems, navigation devices and headphones. The variety of modalities (e.g. visual, auditory, tactile and olfactory) provided by the VR systems, as well as the ability of the VR systems to couple the user's head and even body motions to the projected visual scene and self-avatar (if present), make the VR experience unique and different from passive experiences such as watching television or movies [48]. According to Slater 2009 VR provides *"... a fundamentally different type of experience, with its own unique conventions and possibilities, a medium in which people respond with their whole bodies, treating what they perceive as real..."*[5].

To provide a variety of sensations VR systems use state-of-the-art technologies

VR provides the users with new, alternative form of experiences

---

might be important for research on eating disorders, which shows that young female adults are more likely to engage in disordered eating as compared to young male adults [42, 43].

When describing VR systems there are several terms that need to be clarified. The following list provides a general description of the terms as they are used in the dissertation:

VIRTUAL ENVIRONMENTS (VES) are part of the VR system, which relates specifically to the realism of the projected visual stimuli (the virtual world, including all 3D models and avatars), as well as technical specifications of the projection display, such as field of view (FOV), weight (in case head-mounted), resolution, etc.

IMMERSIVE VIRTUAL ENVIRONMENTS (IVES) can enhance a strong illusion of being in a place different than the current physical environment of the user (see Section 1.3.1 and [5] for more information about immersion). Such an illusion can be induced due to the realistic visual stimuli and display's specifications of the IVE.

VIRTUAL WORLD ³ is the computer graphic generated 3D world, including the 3D spatial layout and 3D models available in the scene.

1.3   VIRTUAL REALITY APPLICATIONS

In general, VR has been mainly used as a tool to simulate the reality [5]. The applications of VR expand to a great variety of fields such as entertainment and visualization, architecture and prototyping, simulations and training, as well as applications for medical or education purposes. The VR tools and technologies have the power to transform the user's sense of body and place, thus creating new forms of experiences [5, 53].

1.3.1   *Entertainment*

Immersion, interaction, intuitiveness, individualization are important components for the successfulness of VR applications used for entertainment purposes

Currently, VR tools and applications are probably mostly used for entertainment, as it provides alternative reality to the users. A typical example of such VR tools are computer games, virtual worlds (e.g. *World of Warcraft* [52]) and location-based entertainment (e.g. *DisneyQuest* [54], *Rocket ship amusement* [50]). Several components of VR have been identified as being crucial for the success of a particular VR application used entertainment purposes [54]:

IMMERSION is a sense that can be enhanced by a system that supports sensorimotor contingencies (a set of valid and meaningful actions/responses to the VE in terms of perception) similar to those of the physical world [5]. Furthermore, *immersion* can be associated with the *place*

---

3 In general, the term *virtual world* is also used to describe interactive and immersive 3D environments that can be used over the Internet by a great number of users to interact at a time [51]. These type of virtual worlds can be divided into two main categories - game-based (Massively Multi-player Online Games, such as *World of Warcraft* [52]) and social worlds, such as *Second Life* [51]. These types of virtual worlds are out of the scope of the research presented in this dissertation.

illusion or the illusion of *being there* (being in the virtual space) [5]. Therefore, *immersion* is related to several characteristics of the VR technology and the connection of the sensorimotor contingencies that the VR system supports to provide an inclusive, extensive, surrounding and vivid illusion of the VE to the user [5], where the illusion is:

- *inclusive* in terms of a lack of awareness of the surrounding physical reality
- *extensive* in terms of accommodated sensory modalities included in the VR system
- *surrounding* in terms of the FOV of the display
- *vivid* in terms of the quality of the 3D content and the resolution of the display

Thus, the characteristics of the *immersive* VR technology are determined by parameters such as frame rate, tracking, latency, display's FOV, quality of graphics of the 3D content in the virtual world [5].

INTERACTION is what makes the experience in VR so unique and different from passively watching a movie for instance. The VR applications should provide intuitive interfaces for controlling the virtual world, including the self-avatars and the interactions with surrounding objects.

INTUITIVE relates to making VR tools easy to use by people from various backgrounds without the need of additional training or explanations. The ultimate goal of VR tools used for mass entertainment is to provide the user with the ability to intuitively figure out how to navigate through the space, interact with objects or use their self-avatar to interact with the VR.

INDIVIDUALIZED relates to making VR applications so that they can fit the needs of each person individually. More specifically, VR applications should have components which enable the user to have individualized experience which matches the user's needs.

1.3.2 *Visualization, prototyping and planning*

Soon after Sutherland developed one of the first VR systems (i.e. *the Ultimate Display* [49]), there have been ideas about possible future implications in architecture [55, 56]. Indeed, currently VR has been used for visualization, prototyping and planning of a variety of design solutions. VR is used to simulate a variety of processes that are useful to be considered before officially starting the building process. Based on the given dimensions of the building and the materials, which the building should be made of, the price for the building can be estimated quite precisely, as well as the amount of time and human resources necessary for the building process. Additionally, interactive visualization of prototypes is used for identifying and fixing problems that cannot be envisioned otherwise during the design process [54]. VR visualization tools are used to evaluate and modify 3D models of design solutions at a lower cost as compared to modifying or building a physical model [57]. Immersive VR tools often provide more realistic experience than tools providing 2D or an overview perspective [54]. One reason for this might be that some cues related to depth and size are not veridically perceived when viewing a prototype in 2D or from an overview perspective. Furthermore, the interactive experience from a 1st PP of the virtual prototype is used to enable the user to explore the space and to simulate an experience of walking around in the virtual space before it is actually built [57].

Immersive VR often provides more realistic experience than 2D tools

1.3.3   Simulations, training and education

Trainings and simulations in the real world are often time-consuming, labor-intensive and limited [47]. The VR is often used to provide trainees the experience of scenarios that cannot be otherwise experienced in a real world setup [6, 7, 9, 58, 59, 60]. In general, most simulation centers provide active training (as a participant). Only a few training centers, such as the Tübinger Patienten-Sicherheits- und Simulations-Zentrum (TuPASS training center, Center for Patient Safety and Simulation [61]), provide also passive training (e.g. debriefing). During the debriefing trainees observe themselves from a 3rd PP through fixed cameras. Trainees report that during the debriefing they learn the most. Probably this is one of the reasons why social perspective-taking in immersive VR scenarios is used for improving team relationships. Some simulation centers use immersive VR applications to provide an opportunity to the practitioners to appreciate the contribution and the expertise of their teammates [62], as well as to observe their own behavior in patient-physician social interactions [63].

VR applications improve training by providing new experiences not possible to simulate in realty

Likewise, my colleagues and I used VR technologies to develop a pipeline for rapid and realistic animation and reconstruction of medical scenarios that can be integrated in an on-line application and used together with real world simulations to improve training effectiveness [6, 7]. The animated scenarios provide the opportunity to the trainees to observe their actions from the perspective of the other participants, such as the other team members or the patient (Figure 1). Such VR applications can be used to further investigate the influence of perspective on perception and training effectiveness for different scenarios.

Since, trainings and simulations should not put any person in risk, VR applications are often used for scenarios which are dangerous to be performed in the real world, such as trainings for nuclear and radiological search [64] or military trainings [9]. Not only the trainee's safety but also the physical capabilities of the actors involved in the scenario are a crucial factor for the realism of the training. For instance, it is not possible for a healthy individual to simulate specific symptoms related to some medical conditions. Often VR trainings involve avatars to simulate patients [6, 7, 58, 59, 60] or civilians [9]. Some simulation centers that use patient simulator systems (e.g. METI [65],

For the trainees VR provides safer, less time-consuming and less labor-intensive training

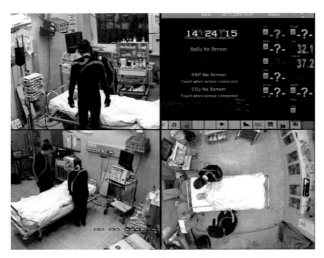

Figure 1: From top left to bottom right: left overview perspective, the monitor with
the patient's vital parameters, right overview perspective and top overview
perspective of a medical training scenario performed in TuPASS training
center. The trainees wear motion capture suits that are part of the Xsens
MVN motion capture system. The body motions of the trainees are captured simultaneously and are used to animate the avatars of the VR application shown in Figure 2 [6, 7].

MSEC[66], SimMan[67]) to provide haptic feedback to trainees are integrat-
ing avatars in their VR tools to provide more realistic visual feedback and
improve the effectiveness of their training programs [6, 58, 59, 60, 62, 68].

1.3.4 *Virtual Reality applications used for medical purposes and education*

In medicine, VR have been used for the visualization of tissues or for teleop-
eration during various medical procedures, such as minimal invasive surgery.
Currently, VR applications are also used for a variety of medical trainings (see
Section 1.3.3), rehabilitations [4], treatment of psychiatric disorders (such as
phobias [69] and anxiety [70, 71]), addiction [72], eating disorders and obesity [12, 13, 73, 74], as well as medical procedures that are known to be very
painful for the patients [8, 48, 75, 76, 77] (see [48] for an overview).

*VR is used for a
variety of medical
applications*

   Researchers found that immersive VR is very effective for reducing pain
[8, 48, 75, 76], while it provides a safe treatment environment (without expos-
ing the patients to any danger) and do not impair the patient's physical therapy
[8]. A reason for this could be that the *immersion* (see Section 1.3.1) provided
by the VR draws away the patient's attention from the reality. Patients often
report a desire to use the VR clinical again [48]. VR applications for distrac-

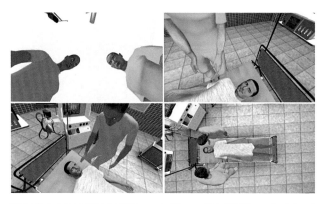

Figure 2: A screenshot from previous work of the candidate ([6, 7]) on animated medical scenarios reconstructed from motion capture and video data. I modeled the 3D hospital-like room in Autodesk 3ds Max 2010® and used the video data (see Figure 1) to reconstruct the scenario. For the medical equipment, I used 3D models from Evermotion 2009©. The VR reconstruction of the medical scenario provides the opportunity to the trainees to observe their actions from the perspective of the other participants (from top left to bottom right): the perspective of the patient, the perspective of the female doctor, the perspective of the male doctor and overview perspective.

tion from painful procedures have been developed not only for adults but also for children [77].

Additionally, researchers suggest that VR applications can be used to help patients suffering from eating disorders and obesity by providing them an alternative experience and allowing them to witness changes in both their shape and behavior [12]. The self-identification with the avatar is important for the effectiveness of many therapies used as a part of a treatment for eating disorders or obesity [12]. However, a limitation of the most of the VR applications is the lack of realistic self-avatars which can be easily modified to match participant in terms of body dimensions and be used in interactive real-time applications [12].

VR is lacking realistic self-avatars that are easy to modify by none-professionals

1.4   AIM OF THIS DISSERTATION

As self-avatars are becoming more popular and largely used in real time VEs for visualization, training and entertainment purposes, it is increasingly important to investigate the influence of the self-avatar on the user's own body perception and perception of the surrounding virtual space. I use novel approaches and state-of-the-art technologies to gain new insights on the way changes of the self-avatar impact perception of body and space in VR. First, I investigate the conditions required for embodying and identifying with a self-avatar of a considerably different body size in immersive VR. This research introduces novel measures to assess embodiment and ownership of a virtual avatar. I propose and use an important methodological novelty for experiments that employ the rubber hand illusion[4] (RHI) paradigm in VR. This novelty provides new insights about: 1) which cues (e.g. visual, proprioceptive, memory, or a combination thereof) influence the participants' body perception; 2) how these cues interact and 3) to what extent each of these cues affects body perception and embodiment.

Further, I investigate the perception of own body weight. First, I consider the mismatch between space perception in the real world and in VR. Therefore, I investigate egocentric distance perception in three LSIDs, as well as the influence of visual depth cues (specifically motion parallax and stereoscopic cues) on the precession of egocentric distances. The findings provide important information that I use for designing the VR setup of the experiment that investigates perception of own body weight. The goal of experiment is to determine the range of weights that individuals accept as their own body weight as portrayed on personalized avatars with varying BMIs. Additionally, I use the unique opportunity that the personalized avatars provide to investigate the relative importance of visual cues, such as the texture and the shape of the self-avatar on body perception.

I use novel approaches and state-of-the-art technologies to investigate how changes in the size of the self-avatar influence perception of body and space in VR

1.5   CONTRIBUTION OF THE CANDIDATE

1.5.1   *Novelties of the dissertation*

This research extends the knowledge about embodiment of a virtual avatar of considerably different body size and introduces novel behavioral response measures (affordances and body size estimations) assessing embodiment (Chapter 5). Unlike the related research, which usually only considers one dimension (only fat distribution of the belly [78], only length [79], only width [80, 81, 82]) when distorting the body size, in this research I use visual stimuli which not only consider the changes in width but also changes in the 3D shape of the entire stylized self-avatar. Another important methodological novelty of this research, not found in the existing literature, is the distinction between the *physical*, the *experienced* and the *virtual* body, which aims to offer a better understanding of which cues (e.g. visual, proprioceptive, memory, or a combination thereof) influence the participants' body perception (see Chapter 5).

My research introduces novel response measures for embodiment and provides new information about embodiment and body perception

To provide useful information for the design of the final experiment, the research presented in this dissertation first investigates the effect of the distance to the target on the precession of egocentric distance estimations in three LSIDs (Chapter 6). First, the experiments presented in Chapter 5 cover more distances than previous experiments, to gain better understanding of the role of the distance to the target on the accuracy of egocentric distance estimates in LSIDs. Second, since most of the studies [20, 22, 83] investigating LSID VEs do not use stereoscopic projection and motion parallax cues in their experimental setup, in one of the LSIDs (the flat LSID) I make a direct

The results of this research have major contribution to space perception in LSID VEs

---
4   see Section 3.1.1 for definition

comparison between the impact of stereoscopic projection and motion parallax on egocentric distance estimates. Even though accessing stereoscopic projection and motion parallax cues across all display types are beyond the scope of this research and also technically not possible, my findings extend the knowledge about the perception of egocentric distances in LSIDs.

Finally, the research presented in Chapter 7 is to my knowledge the first that investigates the range of weights that participants accept as their current weight. It uses a personalized realistic 3D model of the participant with respect to a number of individual specific features, such as fat distribution and postural changes, that vary when weight varies. Further, I take advantage of using 3D models as visual stimuli and decouple texture and geometry (shape) to investigate the relative importance of visual cues, such as texture and shape on body perception.

This research investigates the range of weights accepted as one's current weight and extends the knowledge about the influence of visual cues on the perception of body weight in VR

1.5.2 Contributions to VR applications

The findings of this research can be used to improve VR applications in terms of design and visualization of the 3D content. Also, this research provides new information about the necessary sensory information that a VR system should provide to the user, so that the user can embody even a self-avatar of a considerably different size or perceive the weight of the self-avatar veridically. Thus, this research has implications for VR applications (such as training or entertainment) that use customizable self-avatars and HMD, such as Oculus Rift [84] in which it is important that the user embodies and identifies with their self-avatar. Furthermore, this research has direct implications especially for clinical VR applications [85] and clothing VR tools in which veridical perception of body weight is desired.

This research is important for VR applications, in which embodiment of the self-avatar or veridical perception of body weight is desired

The results are also relevant for the development of new VR therapies to help physicians evaluate the perception of body size perception of patients with body image disorders. More specifically, the procedure used for conducting the body size estimation response measure in the experiments in Chapter 5 and Chapter 7 can be used to inspire new strategies to assess body perception of individuals with eating disorders or stroke.

My research has implications for clinical VR applications

1.5.3 Contribution to body and space perception research in virtual reality

In general, this dissertation provides a major contribution to the body and space perception research in VR. The results provide new general knowledge that could be beneficial for conveying the 3D spatial layout of virtual worlds projected in LSIDs more accurately. The novel findings of this research can be used to enhance the experimental design of studies investigating the 3D spatial layout. This research provides information about the necessary sensory feedback sufficient to induce a sense of agency over the virtual self-avatar of considerably different size. The methodological novelty that I introduce in Chapter 5 can be used to collect estimations based on specific cues that influence body perception in VR. My research shows that personalized avatars

The findings can be used to enhance experimental design and provide new insights about body perception in VR

can be used to investigate body perception in VR in a way that has not been used so far, namely by investigating the contribution of visual cues to body perception.

1.5.4   Declaration of the contribution of the candidate

At the time of the submission of this PhD thesis[5], the ideas and the results of the presented research have been already published in three journal articles, listed by the descending date of publishing:

The candidate published the research presented in this PhD thesis in three journal articles

IVELINA V. PIRYANKOVA, Jeanine K. Stefanucci, Javier Romero, Stephan de la Rosa, Michael J. Black, and Betty J. Mohler. **Can I recognize my body's weight? The influence of shape and texture on the perception of self.** *ACM Trans. Appl. Percept.*, 11(3): 13:1 13:18, September 2014. ISSN 1544-3558. doi: 10.1145/2641568. (Chapter 7) (Presented as a talk and chosen as one of the five **best papers** in the Symposium on Applied Perception 2014, and therefore invited and presented as a poster at **SIGGRAPH 2014**, Canada, Vancouver)

IVELINA V. PIRYANKOVA, Hong Yu Wong, Sally A. Linkenauger, Catherine Stinson, Matthew R. Longo, Heinrich H. Bülthoff, and Betty J. Mohler. **Owning an overweight or underweight body: Distinguishing the physical, experienced and virtual body.** *PLoS ONE*, 9:e103428, August 2014. (Chapter 5)

IVELINA V. PIRYANKOVA, Stephan de la Rosa, Uwe Kloos, Heinrich H. Bülthoff and Betty J. Mohler, **Egocentric distance perception in large screen immersive displays**, *Displays*, 34(2):153-164, April 2013. (Chapter 6)

As indicated by the fact that the PhD candidate is a first author of each one of them, the ideas for the studies in Chapter 5, 6, 7 were proposed by the candidate. Stimulus generation[6] was predominantly carried out by the candidate. The stylized avatar used in this research is part of the Complete Characters Library HD of Rocketbox Studios GmbH [87]. The stylized avatar was modified by the candidate for the purpose of the research. The personalized avatars used in this research are generated (see Section 7.1.2) by the research group of Prof. Dr. Michael Black from Perceiving Systems at Max-Planck-Institute (MPI) for Intelligent Systems in Tübingen [88]. For the purpose of the research the candidate developed a pipeline for using the personalized avatars in real-time immersive VR setups (see Section 7.1.3). The design, experimental work and the analysis of all results have been predominantly carried out by the candidate. The co-authors role for conducting the presented research was that of supervision, giving advice and offering criticism, as well as revising the listed manuscripts.

Previous related research of the candidate is used to provide examples of animation pipelines and clinical VR applications

---

5 See [86] to find the LaTeX template used in this dissertation
6 In Sections 2.3, 5.1.3 and 7.1.3 I explain in more detail the techniques and the software which I used

In Section 1.3.3 and Chapter 2 previous research carried out and published by the candidate is outlined to provide examples of a clinical VR application and pipeline for animating state-of-the-art stylized and personalized self-avatars:

IVELINA V. ALEXANDROVA, Marcus Rall, Martin Breidt, Uwe Kloos, Gabriella Tullius, Heinrich H. Bülthoff, and Betty J. Mohler. **Animations of medical training scenarios in immersive virtual environments.** *In Digital Media and Digital Content Management (DMDCM),* Workshop on IEEE Computer Society Washington, pages 912, May 2011. doi: 10.1109/DMDCM.2011.64.

IVELINA V. ALEXANDROVA, M. Rall, M. Breidt, G. Tullius, U. Kloos, H.H. Bülthoff, and B.J. Mohler. **Enhancing medical communication training using motion capture, perspective taking and virtual reality.** *In 19th Medicine Meets Virtual Reality Conference: NextMed (MMVR 2012),* pages 1622, February 2012.

IVELINA V. ALEXANDROVA, Paolina T. Teneva, Stephan de la Rosa, Uwe Kloos, Heinrich H. Bülthoff, and Betty J. Mohler. **Egocentric distance judgments in a large screen display immersive virtual environment.** *In Proceedings of the 7th Symposium on Applied Perception in Graphics and Visualization (APGV 2010),* pages 5760, New York, NY, USA, 2010. ACM.

2

STATE-OF-THE-ART REALISTIC AVATARS AND IMMERSIVE DISPLAYS TECHNOLOGIES

This chapter presents state-of-the-art realistic avatars and immersive displays technologies used in VR tools, as well as approaches and technologies that I have used for generating the visual stimuli used in my research. First, I introduce the common pipeline used for creating and animating state-of-the-art self-avatars, which contains three main processes. Specifically, the current state-of-the-art methods for creating realistic avatars include either artistic drawings or 3D scanning technology (Section 2.1.1 and 2.1.2). Once the avatar is created, often it is animated with predefined motions or the user's own motions in real-time (Section 2.1.4). Finally, a VR programming software is used to visualize the self-avatar in the VE (Section 2.2). Then, I outline state-of-the-art immersive displays technologies used for the visualization of VEs (Section 2.4).

2.1 STATE-OF-THE-ART REALISTIC AVATARS

Self-avatars should match the user's expectations [89, 90, 91]. Depending on the purpose of the VR application they could possess features, which have different level of realism of motions, appearance and interaction with the surrounding space.

2.1.1 Creating stylized avatars

Generally, the avatars used to represent the user's body in the virtual world are stylized avatars. These avatars are based on artists' drawings often inspired by real humans. Typical examples of stylized avatars are the avatars used in computer games. Many virtual worlds, games and applications allow the user to customize the appearance of the stylized avatars by giving the user the ability to choose different properties of the avatar, such as gender, age, race, hair or dressing style. The customizable avatars enable the user to create a number of identities which may often be considerably different than the user's off-line identity [51] [92, p.184].

Stylized avatars are based on artists' drawings

Self-avatars are used on a regular basis to represent people not only in gaming applications but also in a variety of VR applications, for example in business or organizational meetings [51]. Researchers found that men prefer to pick taller and larger avatars than women would pick, while women prefer thinner avatars [93]. Dunn et al. 2012 also found that the discrepancy between the avatar and the user is related to self-esteem. Thus, people with low self-esteem have greater discrepancy between their own appearance and that of their avatar, as compared to people with higher self-esteem [93].

2.1.2   *Creating personalized avatars*

Personalized avatars are generated using data, based on 3D scans of real humans

Although in many VR applications and virtual worlds it is not necessary for the customized avatars to resemble the user in any way, there are a great number of VR applications (e.g. clinical VR or ergonomics) in which the similarity with the user is preferable [12]. Especially, when the aim of the VR application (e.g. [94]) is to provide feedback to the user related to their body shape or appearance. Therefore, the use of personalized avatars is growing increasingly. Personalized avatars are created from 3D scans of real humans. Thus, the avatars possess the individual's specific features, such as body dimensions, skin particularities or fat distribution. However, it is also possible to embed some of the individual's specific features, such as height or limb length, to an stylized character (see Chapter 5).

Due to the rapid development of technology and the low-cost 3D scanning systems (such as Microsoft's Kinect sensor [95]), it is now possible to capture the users body shape even at home and based on the person's body morphology to create a self-avatar. More sophisticated depth scanning systems are also used for a variety of health care and non-health care purposes, such as body research [38], surgical simulations [96], clothing fit [97], etc. [98].

Full body 3D scanning systems capture texture and geometry

An example of such a system is the custom full body 3D stereo capture system at the Perceiving Systems department from MPI for Intelligent Systems build by 3dMD (Atlanta, GA) [99] (Figure 3). The system is composed of 22 stereo units each equipped with a pair of black and white cameras and a 5*megapixel* color camera. The black an white cameras observe the textured light pattern projected by speckle projectors and are used for capturing the shape. The 5*megapixel* color camera captures the body texture. The system provides very good coverage of the human body in different poses, and can resolve the 3D locations of a point on the body to approximately 1*mm*. The system was used to capture the 3D scans of the participants used for generating the personalized avatars in the research of Chapter 7.

Full body 4D scanning systems capture 3D shape over time

Furthermore, there are scanning systems which are capable of capturing not only the texture and the shape but also the dynamic deformations of the 3D mesh over time. An example of such system is the 4D dynamic full body scanner at the Perceiving Systems department from MPI for Intelligent Systems [100]. The 4D scanning system is used to capture the deformations of human bodies in motion, by capturing the body shape at 60 frame per second. This unique system is built built by 3dMD (Atlanta, GA) and uses 22 pairs of stereo cameras, 22 color cameras, and custom speckle projectors [100] to capture body motions [100].

2.1.3   *Static self-avatars*

Static self-avatars are often used VR applications, which provide head tracking

Static self-avatars are not animated with the user's motions. Still static self-avatars are often used in VR applications. Usually the pose of the self-avatar is a general pose, one that the user might take when using the VR application. Due to the capabilities of current technologies, many VR applications that use

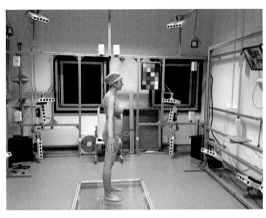

Figure 3: A person preparing for a 3D scan in the full body 3D stereo capture system, at the Perceiving Systems department from the MPI for Intelligent Systems.

$1^{st}PP$ self-avatars with static bodies visualize the HMD VE using the position and orientation from the user's head tracking data to update the projected visual stimuli respectively.

2.1.4   Animating self-avatars in real-time

Several years ago most of the self-avatars of VR applications were static, mainly because of the high-cost tracking systems and devices, as well as the complexity of the pipelines necessary for the animation process. Currently, VR applications have animation pipelines which use low-cost devices like Microsoft's Kinect sensor [95] and the Leap Motion [101] to animate the user's self-avatars with the user's motions. Furthermore, pipelines for rapid (within several minutes) generation of personalized avatars such as the one developed by Shapiro et al. [102] make it now possible to semi-automatically generate, rig and skin a personalized avatar, which can be used in a real-time 3D VE. Shapiro et al. [102] use the Microsoft's Kinect sensor [95] to create the mesh and the texture of the personalized avatar. The fact that such avatars possess user's specific features (e.g. cloths, proportions, skin color) may contribute to more immersive experience for the users of VR applications.

2.1.4.1   Methods for animating self-avatars in real-time

The common state-of-the-art pipeline for the animation of avatars involves a precise mapping between the user's motions and the skinned and rigged mesh of the avatar (stylized or personalized), so that each joint of the motion data corresponds to a joint on the skinned and rigged mesh. Initially the 3D mesh of the avatar only describes its geometry but does not have any bones that

The 3D mesh describes the geometry of the 3D model

are related to it (Figure 4). The bones are generally another structure (biped) composed of several meshes (one for each bone). The structure of bones can be rigged to create a skeleton and make controls, which can later enable the animators to animate the skeleton or can be used to apply a pre-recorded or real-time animation (motion tracking data). The skinning provides the relation between each vertex of the 3D mesh with a particular bone of the rigged skeletal structure. Thus, the part of the skinned mesh attached to the bone moves along with the bone. Therefore, each vertex of the mesh should be assigned to at least one bone. In order to make the motions realistic vertices are often assigned to two or more neighboring bones. In case a vertex of the mesh does not get assigned to a bone, its position and orientation in the 3D space will remain the same during the entire animation. The motions of the mesh will appear unrealistic due to stretched edges between the unassigned vertex and the neighboring vertices.

The skeleton is a rigged structure of bones (3D meshes)

The skinning provides the relation between each vertex (in the mesh) with a bone (in the skeleton)

Figure 4: A mesh of a personalized avatar extracted from a 3D scan data of a person. The mesh is generated by the research group of Prof. Dr. Michael Black from Perceiving Systems at MPI for Intelligent Systems in Tübingen.

2.1.4.2   *Animating self-avatars using motion capture data*

Most often the avatars used in VR applications are animated using body motion capture data. Some applications also use face motions (e.g. [103], [104], [105]) or hand gestures in addition to body motions to animate the avatars. Capturing the user's motions is done using motion capture systems[1], such as Vicon [107] or Xsens MVN [108] or skeletal tracking sensors like Kinect [95] or Leap Motion [101]. The low-cost of commercial skeletal tracking sensors (e.g. Kinect [95], Leap Motion [101]) makes it possible for the users to

---

1 More detailed information about optical, magnetic or mechanical motion capture systems is provided in the master thesis [36] of the candidate, as well as in the report of Furniss Dec. 1999

animate their self-avatars when playing computer games or use other VR applications at home. These sensors are also often used for research purposes as well.

2.1.4.3 *State-of-the-art optical motion tracking system*

The experiments presented in this dissertation use a state-of-the-art optical motion tracking system (Vicon [107]). The optical tracking system uses 16 high-speed motion capture cameras (Vicon MX13) and Vicon Tracker 1.2 software to track a space of $11.9m \times 11.7m$. Each Vicon camera has a resolution of $1280 pixels \times 1024 pixels$. The motion tracking system transmits the tracked data via the Virtual-Reality Peripheral Network protocol to the graphics visualization system using a wireless connection. The received data can be used to visualize in real-time the VE (including self-avatars). The generated visual image corresponds to the user's body and head motions in the real world. The system tracks the user's motions by using cameras emitting infrared light and monitoring the position and orientation of reflective markers, balls of different sizes[2], that reflect the infra-red light back to the cameras. Depending on the purpose and the specifications of the VR application, the reflective markers could be attached either:

Optical motion capture provides absolute position and orientation of the tracking data

- directly to the user's skin, for instance, to capture face motions for animating the face of the user's self-avatar.

- to a tight suit that the user wears (Figure 5) to capture body motions for animating the body of the user's self-avatar. However, when animating several users in real-time one should consider that due to the interaction between the users some markers may often be occluded. In case the pipeline for real-time animation is not robust enough, the occlusion of the markers may hinder the realism of the avatars' animations. Even if reflective markers are occluded during the motion capture session, the data can usually be fixed in the process of the animation post-processing. Therefore, often both optical and magnetic motion capture systems are used in combination to provide more reliable data (Figure 6). The reason for this is that optical tracking systems provide great accuracy due to the absolute position and orientation of the avatar with respect to the surrounding environment. At the same time the data from the magnetic motion capture system provides accurate information about the relative position of the body parts of the avatar with respect to each other (Figure 6). Thus the movements of two users can be simultaneously captured by two Xsens MVN magnetic motion capture systems (e.g. Alexandrova et al. 2011 and Alexandrova et al. 2012) (Figure 2). Another possibility (only applicable for post-processed animations) is to use a video data to synchronize and adjust the avatars for more details see Alexandrova et al. 2011 and Alexandrova et al. 2012).

Optical motion tracking is done by attaching reflective markers to the performer's body or to a rigid object attached to the performer's body parts, such as head or feet

---

2 The reflective markers used for body motion capture are usually bigger that the markers used for face motion capture. The size of the markers depends also on the resolution of the particular system.

- to rigid objects that the user wears. The rigid object is a unique config-uration of several reflective markers fixed to an object, such as HMD, gloves, belt, shoes. The reflective markers are positioned so that the distance between each other is always constant. The rigid objects at-tached to a HMD (Figure 6) are usually used to track the user's head motions. The tracking data is used by the visualization system to update the user's position and orientation in the VE and projects the VE in the HMD respectively, thus generating a visual image of the VE which cor-responds to the user's motions in the real world. Likewise, rigid objects attached to the body parts (arms and feet) of the users can be used for animating self-avatars with inverse kinematics (e.g. [40]). Due to the unique shape of the tracked rigid objects the system allows tracking of multiple users and projects the virtual scene and animates the user's self-avatars in real-time respectively.

Figure 5: A person participating in a body motion capture session using an optical motion capture system (Vicon). The performer is wearing a tight suit cov-ered with reflective markers for capturing the body motions.

2.1.4.4   State-of-the-art inertial and magnetic motion capture

An example of a state-of-the-art inertial and magnetic motion capture system is Xsens MVN. Similar to the other magnetic motion capture systems, the Xsens MVN uses magnetic receivers and transmitters to track the user's rel-ative position and orientation. The system uses 17 inertial sensors (receivers, each equipped with a 3D gyroscope, a 3D accelerometer and a 3D magne-tometer) connected in an array with two Masters and integrated in an suit [109]. The Masters exchange data between the receivers and the transmitter [109]. For this reason the system is only accurate in terms of relative posi-tion and orientation, but not with respect to the user's absolute position and orientation in space (e.g. the users position with respect to the other user).

Inertial and magnetic motion capture provide relative position and orientation of the tracked object

Figure 6: A person looking down to see her animated self-avatar in VR. The person wears Xsens MVN motion capture suit, which captures her body motions. The rigid object attached to the belt is coupled to the pelvis of the self-avatar and is used to provide absolute position and orientation of the person's body in space. The rigid object attached to the HMD is used to track the user's head position and orientation in space. Thus the VR system updates the VE according to person's head motions.

Additionally, the receivers use wireless transmission to connect with the Xsens MVN software. The user can relatively freely move in indoor and outdoor spaces. Still, the user's range of motion is limited to the range of the transmitter connected with wire to the graphics visualization system [106]. As the distance between the receivers and the transmitters increases, the data gets noisier, usually due to drift and magnetic interference. The motion captured data is streamed in real-time and can be visualized in the Xsens MVN software as well as in platforms like Virtools 5.0 (3DVIA Dassault Systemes©) and Unity 3D. Thus, the data can be used for animating a self-avatar in real-time (Figure 6).

2.1.4.5 *Calibration*

To minimize errors and maximize accuracy of the motion captured data, motion capture systems should ideally be calibrated before each capture session. Thus, the system can determine the user's dimensions and range of motion in a more reliable way. A typical pose used for calibration is a pose, in which the person stands upright with horizontally spread arms and the thumbs pointed forward (T-pose) (Figure 5). The range of motion usually is determined by the motions that the user is going to perform during the motion capture session. To track the motions as accurately as possible the suit to which the markers

Calibration is used to minimize errors and maximize accuracy of the captured data

are attached should be tight and the markers should stay fixed during the entire motion capture session. For the magnetic motion capture systems, such as Xsens MVN the user's dimensions (height, foot size, arm length) can be used as an input for greater precision of the motion capture data. For the optical motion capture system it is important that each marker is visible for the system at any point of time.

2.2   PLATFORMS FOR VISUALIZING SELF-AVATARS AND CREATING 3D INTERACTIVE TOOLS

For programming the interactive VEs used in the experiments presented in this dissertation I have used two commonly used visualization platforms for creating 3D interactive applications, namely:

For programming the interactive VEs the candidate used Virtools 5.0 and Unity 3D

VIRTOOLS 5.0 (3DVIA DASSAULT SYSTEMES©) used for programming the experiments presented in Chapter 5 and Chapter 6. In Chapter 5 Virtools 5.0 was used for programming the scripts that set some properties of the VE such as the size of the avatar and the distance between the poles based on an input file, or scripts used to adjust, for instance, the length of the body parts of the avatar to match the participant or the body size of the avatar and the distance between the poles with a joypad. In Chapter 6 Virtools 5.0 was used to set the position of the target based on an input file and to update the visual scene based on the head motions of the participant.

UNITY 3D was used for programming the experiment presented in Chapter 7 and setting the scene in which the mesh of the personalized avatar was loaded.

2.3   TOOLS FOR CREATING AND ANIMATING COMPUTER GRAPHICS CONTENT

Currently there are powerful tools available, that are used to design, build, texture and rig sophisticated digital content, which can then be realistically animated and rendered in real-time with stunning visual effects. Tools for 3D graphics production like Autodesk 3ds Max [110], Autodesk Maya [110] and Blender [111], are used by millions of users to create their own 3D computer graphics content. I have used Autodesk 3ds Max [110] to model and modify the 3D content used in this dissertation.

For modeling the 3D content of the VEs and modifying the avatars used in this dissertation the candidate used Autodesk 3ds Max

I have modeled the realistic VEs for each of the experiments. To increase the realism of the VE the textures and the materials of the 3D models are extracted from photographs of the real objects. Additionally, I rendered ambient occlusion maps and light maps for some of the static objects and added additional lighting to provide realistic shadows of the dynamic objects in the VE (Figure 2).

The stylized self-avatars that I used in this research have been created by Rocketbox Studios GmbH [87] and are part of their Complete Characters Library HD. In order to use this stylized avatars for the purpose of my research I modified the body shape of a female avatar so that through the shape change and the difference in fat distribution of the same avatar differences in weight can be portrayed (Figure 7. Chapter 5 provides more details about the modifications made to the avatar.

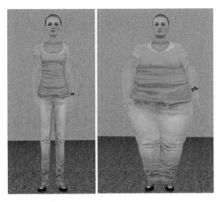

Figure 7: A rendering of the modified stylized avatar from Rocketbox Studios GmbH: left - underweight; right - overweight.

The personalized avatars used in this research are generated by the research group of Prof. Dr. Michael Black from Perceiving Systems at MPI for Intelligent Systems in Tübingen [88]. A short description of their pipeline is provided in Chapter 7. The research of Hirshberg et al. 2012, Bogo et al. 2014 and Weiss et al. 2011 provides more detailed information of the different components of the pipeline. Still, for the purpose of my research I generated a morphable mesh for each of the personalized avatars used in the experiment presented in Chapter 7. The morphable mesh uses the participants original 3D mesh and eight deformed versions of the original mesh to ensure that every mesh has identical morphs and specifications, I programmed a script which makes the morphing process automatic in Autodesk 3ds Max Script [110]. The morphing is based on blend shapes. Blend shapes is a technique which is used to interpolate between meshes with identical vertices but of different shapes.

Blend shapes is a morphing technique which is used to interpolate between meshes with identical vertices but of different shapes

2.4 TYPES OF IMMERSIVE DISPLAY TECHNOLOGIES USED IN VR SYSTEMS

As mentioned in Chapter 1 immersive displays are used to visualized the 3D content of the VE to the user of VR applications. Therefore, immersive displays technologies (e.g. *Sensorama* [47]) and envisions of such technologies (e.g. *the ultimate display* [49]) exists ever since the beginning of VR. The technological advances in VR systems are closely related to the technological development of immersive displays. Currently, there is a great number of immersive display used in the state-of-the-art VR systems. In general, immersive displays can be divided into three main categories [115], namely:

There are three main categories of immersive displays, namely small-, medium- and large-scale immersive displays

SMALL-SCALE IMMERSIVE DISPLAYS are displays used by a single user, such as HMDs and desktop stereoscopic displays [115].

MEDIUM-SCALE IMMERSIVE DISPLAYS are displays that can be used by small groups of people and provide multi-user collaboration, such as CAVEs [116], curved screen displays (semi-spherical LSID, flat LSID) and power walls,

LARGE-SCALE IMMERSIVE DISPLAYS [3] are displays designed to provide an immersive experience of large groups (up to hundreds) of people, such as IMAX and wide field-of-view domes [117].

In the field of body and space perception research in VR the small- and medium-scale immersive displays are generally used. Likewise, the research presented in this thesis uses immersive displays from these two categories. Therefore, the rest of the section provides more detailed information about the state-of-the-art of HMDs and LSIDs.

2.4.1   *Head-mounted displays*

HMDs became widely popular in the last several years with the Oculus Rift, an immersive VR headset for computer games [84]. However, HMD technologies exist at least since the early 1960's with the invention of the *Telesphere mask* [46] and the 3D HMD [118]. HMDs are highly immersive mostly because they are designed in a way that the user can barely see something other than the projected virtual world. The projection screens of the HMDs are positioned right in front of the user's eyes. Additionally, to ensure that the physical environment is blocked from view, HMDs often have a black cloth or plastic surrounding their projection screens.

Due to their design HMDs are highly immersive

Two of the most generally used state-of-the-art HMDs in the field of body and space perception research in VR are:

THE NVISOR SX60 has a FOV of $44°$ horizontal and $35°$ vertical FOV per eye, a resolution of $1280 pixels \times 1024 pixels$ per eye and weights $1kg$ according to the manufacturer [119], a refresh rate of 60 Hz per eye. The nVisor SX60 is commonly used in space perception research (e.g. the research of McManus et al. 2011, Mohler et al. 2008, Williams et al. [121]).

THE NVISOR SX111 has a stereoscopic wide FOV with $76°$ horizontal and $64°$ vertical FOV per eye, a resolution of $1280 pixels \times 1024 pixels$ per eye, a refresh rate of 60 Hz per eye. The user can adjust interpupillary distance (IPD) for their needs. Since it has been shown that measuring and adjusting the IPD for each participant does not significantly

---

3 See the research of Lantz 2007 and 1998 for an overview of large-scale immersive displays.

improve participant's perception in HMDs up to $15m$ [122], I used the average IPD ($6.5cm$) for all participants. The weight of nVisor SX111 is approximately $1.3kg$ according to the manufacturer [123]. The nVisor SX111 is used in body perception research in VR (e.g. the research of Kilteni et al. 2013).

The nVisor SX111 was used in experiment presented in Chapter 5 because it provides the wider FOV. I considered the weight of the nVisor SX111 when designing the experiment.

The nVisor SX111 was used in experiment presented in Chapter 5

2.4.2 *Large screen immersive displays*

In contrast to HMDs, LSIDs enable the users to see their own body or real tools while looking at the VE. LSIDs are often custom made for the specific purpose of the setup (see Ni et al. 2006 for detailed descriptions of various LSIDs and example applications). Also, the technical aspects of LSIDs often vary in many ways. LSIDs can be plane projecting surfaces or displays merged with stages to enable the creation of dynamic environments, transformed by the projected media (e.g. location-based entertainment [54]). LSIDs can vary in shape (flat, curved, e.g. the Dish [125] or completely enclosed cave automatic virtual environment (CAVE) [116]), the number of the projection surfaces, the ability to track the position of the user and the availability of stereoscopic projection.

The design of the LSIDs allows the user to see their physical body while viewing the VE

The difference in specifications of the projection setup influences their ability to convey visual cues providing depth information (see Thompson et al. 2005 and Cutting et al. 1995 for summary chapters). More specifically, focus cues (see Section 3.2.2) are influenced by the distance between the viewer and the projection surface. The ability to track the position of the observer's head in real-time is necessary for cues such as motion parallax (see Section 3.2.2). In summary, different combinations of visual cues provided by the technical setup of the LSID may create a different perceptual experience of depth. Still, all displays share common features such as the center of projection (CoP) for instance. These CoP is located in front of the display in a certain distance from the center of the display (for more detailed information about the calculation of the CoP see Vishwanath et al. [127]). The CoP is the location from which the viewer can most accurately perceive the 3D layout of a virtual scene projected in a given display [127, 128, 129]. Therefore, it is helpful to use the CoP as a viewing position when evaluating depth perception in a variety of LSIDs.

The different combinations of visual cues provided by the technical setup of the LSID may create a different perceptual experience of depth

Three LSIDs have been used for the research presented in this dissertation

For conducting the research presented in Chapters 6 and 7 I have used the following three of the LSIDs:

SEMI-SPHERICAL LSID [4] had four JVC© D-ILADLASX21S video projectors each with a resolution of $1400pixels \times 1050pixels$ at the time when the experiment presented in Chapter 6 was conducted. The visual stimuli are projected on the front, the sides, and the floor of a custom made semi-spherical LSID. The projection surface enables a FOV of $220°$ horizontal and $165°$ vertical. The setup of the LSID does not provide stereoscopic projection and motion parallax (see Chapter 6, Figure 20).

MPI CABIN LSID is a part of the Cybermotion simulator. The LSID has two EYEVIS© (see [130]) video projectors with a resolution of $1920pixels \times 1200pixels$ (see Masone et al. [131] for more technical details). The visual stimuli are projected on the front and the sides of the MPI cabin LSID. The projection surface of the MPI cabin LSID enables a FOV of $140°$ horizontal by $70°$ vertical. The MPI cabin LSID does not yet support stereoscopic projection nor tracking of the participant's head position and orientation, therefore stereo cues and motion parallax were not provided (see Chapter 6, Figure 21).

FLAT LSID uses one Christie SX+ video projector with a resolution of $1400pixels \times 1050pixels$. Thus the visual stimuli are projected on a plane in front of the participant which covers an area of $2.16m \times 1.62m$. The projection surface enables a FOV of $105°$ horizontal and $88°$ vertical from a viewing distance to the screen of $0.83m$ (as used in Chapter 6) and 94.4 horizontal and 78 vertical from a viewing distance of $1m$ (as used in Chapter 7). The projection plane of the flat LSID is located at $0.265m$ above the real floor. To provide motion parallax and stereoscopic depth cues in the flat LSID in Chapter 6 I used a Vicon motion tracking system, which uses four Vicon V-series cameras. For the research in Chapter 7) the tracking system was up graded and currently the setup uses a ART © SMARTTRACK motion tracking system, which includes two tracking cameras. For both systems a rigid object with reflective markers was used to track the user's head motions and the generated stereoscopic projection used IPD of $0.065m$ [132]. In order to see the VE stereoscopically the viewer had to wear NVIDIA© shutter glasses (see Figure 8). The design of the shutter glasses is similar to that of regular glasses. The shutter glasses had a horizontal FOV of 103 and vertical FOV of 62, which covered an area of about $2.52m \times 1.2m$ of the flat LSID when viewed from a distance of $1m$.

---

4 Currently the setup of the semi-spherical LSID has been updated. The projection now has six EYEVIS LED DLP projectors (each $1920pixels \times 1200pixels$, 60Hz). Five projectors are rotated by $90°$ horizontally to cover the projection surface on the walls of the LSID. Additionally, one projector projects on the floor of the semi-spherical LSID. The projectors are LED-based. The rendering is done on a cluster system.

Figure 8: A participant viewing the stereoscopically projected VE in the flat LSID wearing NVIDIA© shutter glasses.

2.5 LIMITATIONS

Considering the outlined state-of-the-art displays technologies and pipelines for generating realistic avatars used for visualization of VEs, both still have limitations. Some of the general limitations that LSIDs have concern the FOV, the surface reflection or the contrast of the projection [117]. For instance, many LSIDs provide a wide horizontal FOV, but the vertical FOV seems to be more important for the sense of immersion [54]. Only a few LSID support projection on the floor under the user's feet (Figure 20), while most of the LSIDs project the VE on the wall in front of the user (Figure 22). On the other hand, due to their ergonomics HMDs isolate people from the others and the real world [54]. This might be beneficial for the sense of immersion in the VE, while it is not always preferable especially for face to face communication. HMDs also have limited FOV and the user's feel the weight of the HMD.

Both HMDs and LSIDs have practical limitations mainly related to their design and technical specifications

The user's physical body in HMDs is not visible, while in LSIDs the user's are able to see their body while looking at the VE. Additionally, both stylized and personalized self-avatars have a number of limitations. Stylized self-avatar are currently more popular than the personalized self-avatars. The shape of the stylized self-avatars is often cartoon-like and idealized in a sense that it does not necessarily represents the general proportions of an average human body. These differences between the stylized self-avatars as compared to humans may contribute to the fact that most animated stylized self-avatars ap-

The state-of-the-art methods for animating the self-avatars still have practical limitations

pear realistic. Considering the *uncanny valley* theory[5] proposed by Mori 1970 personalized avatars may appear appear creepy, unnatural or uncanny if they do not act like real humans. The reason for this is similarity between humans and their personalized avatars. Animating personalized avatars is challenging mainly because current real-time motion capture and animation pipelines do not yet capture and animate motions like swallowing or breathing, which might be crucial for the realistic appearance of the personalized avatars.

Additionally, unrealistic animation of the personalized avatars might bias the user's perception in many different ways including their perception of visual cues and the size of the avatar. Furthermore, the implications of the PhD thesis target a great number of VR applications that not always support pipelines for animating the user's self-avatar. Therefore, animated personalized self-avatars are beyond the scope of the research presented in this thesis.

---

5 The *uncanny valley* theory suggests that the user's expectations should be matched in terms of the appearance and the range of motions of the robot or the avatar, otherwise the avatar will appear creepy and uncanny.

3

RELATED RESEARCH

This chapter outlines body and space perception literature related to the research presented in this PhD thesis. First, I present body perception research by providing information about embodiment and body perception, as well as response measures and methods used to assess perception of body size. In the second part of this section I introduce several different research areas related to space perception.

3.1 BODY PERCEPTION AND EMBODIMENT

Before I introduce the literature related to body perception and embodiment, I would like to define relevant terms that I will use throughout this dissertation:

BODY MORPHOLOGY is a term which describes the size, the shape, the structure and the relationship between the body parts, as well as features (e.g. color and proportions) which distinguish specific individuals and make them unique [133].

BODY DIMENSIONS are the metric properties of the body, the shape and the proportions. Features that are properties of the individual's texture, such as skin color or wrinkles, are not part of the body dimensions.

BODY SHAPE is the geometry of the body.

BODY IMAGE is the mental, multi-modal perceptual, conceptual, or emotional representation of one's own body, which involves sensory inputs perceived through 1st person experience and through the experience of the body as an object in the physical world [37, 74, 134, 135, 136]. The findings of recent research (see Section 3.1.4) suggest that even healthy participants perceive a mismatch between their actual body size and their body image, albeit not as much as patients with eating disorders [82, 137, 138].

BODY SIZE is an aspect of body image, which refers to the overall body dimensions.

SENSE OF OWNERSHIP is an illusion whereby people perceive non-corporal objects such as artificial limbs as parts of their own body. [139, 140, 141, 142, 143]. In reality people normally only feel a sense of ownership over their own body and its parts.

EMBODIMENT is an illusion that can be divided into several subcomponents, including senses of ownership, agency and location [142, 143, 144].

3.1.1 *Embodiment of artificial limbs in reality*

The RHI is a paradigm in which people experience a sense of ownership over an artificial limb, such as a rubber hand

Most investigations of body ownership employ the RHI paradigm [140, 141] (see [142] for an overview). Generally in RHI experiments, the participant sits with their hands resting on a table in front of them. One of the participant's hands is blocked from view, and a rubber hand is positioned on the table between the unseen hand and the midpoint between the participant's hands. A sense of ownership over the rubber hand can be induced by applying synchronous visual-tactile stimulation by simultaneously touching or stroking the seen rubber hand and the unseen real hand [141, 142]. Synchronous multisensory stimulation over one body part can even extend to ownership over the entire body [145]. Also, it has been shown that multisensory illusions can be induced with synchronous visual-motor stimulation without the need for passive touch [139, 146, 147]. However, if the visual-tactile stimulation is asynchronous (the visual stimulation is not synchronous with the touch or the stroking), a sense of ownership is typically not induced [142]. In addition, RHI occurs if the posture of the rubber hand and the participant's own hand match and they are positioned in a similar way [141, 148]. To quantify the effect of body ownership the researchers use the following three main types of response measures: 1) subjective measures, such as self-reports in terms of questionnaires provided to the participants after the stimulation (both synchronous and asynchronous) [78, 80, 143, 149, 150]; 2) physiological measures, such as heart-rate [149] or skin conductance [80, 151] (measured before and after the stimulation) and 3) behavioral measures, such as matching tasks [151], proprioceptive drift [152], or size drift in perceived size of body parts [78, 79] (measured before and after the stimulation). Generally, after synchronous stimulation the participants report significantly stronger agreement with the statements of the questionnaires as compared to their self-reports after asynchronous stimulation [78, 80, 143, 149, 150]. Similar to the self-reports the physiological and the behavioral measures indicate significantly stronger change between the pre and the post measure in the synchronous condition as compared to the asynchronous condition.

A sense of ownership over an artificial limb can be induced by applying synchronous visual-tactile stimulation to both the seen rubber hand and the unseen real hand

There are three main main types of response measures used to quantify the effect of body ownership: subjective, physiological and behavioral measures

3.1.2 *Embodiment in virtual reality applications*

Many researchers use the potential of VR to investigate body perception and more specifically the plasticity of body representation in immersive HMD VEs [78, 79, 149, 153, 154]. Lenggenhager et al. [152] used the RHI paradigm in a VR experiment to induce an illusion of body ownership that involves the whole body. Petkova and Ehrsson [80] showed that their participants experienced a body swap with the experimenter after seeing themselves shake hands with the experimenter from the experimenter's perspective. Some scientists suggest that in a VE, it is not only visually and spatially synchronous touch that can induce a body ownership illusion, but also synchronous sensory-motor stimulation [78, 79], head tracking [149], or seeing the body from 1st PP [149, 155].

Using the RHI paradigm Normand et al. [78] showed that participants perceive their belly to be bigger after synchronous visual-tactile stimulation. Van der Hoort et al. [151] used legs which were significantly different in size from the legs of their participants and found that after synchronous visual-tactile stimulation, participants felt ownership over the legs. Additionally, the size of the embodied legs had an influence on the perceived size and distance to objects [151]. Kilteni et al. [79] provided synchronous sensory-motor stimulation of a virtual hand which was a of a considerably different length than participants' real hands, and found that participants experienced ownership over the virtual hand. Preston et al. [81] found that illusory ownership over a large body does not have an effect on the perceived body width, while ownership over a slimmer body caused a significant decrease in the participant's perceived body width.

The body dimensions of the embodied self-avatar in VR can influence the felt body size, width, length, shape and symmetry, as well as size and distance to objects

Slater et al. [149] demonstrated that male participants can feel ownership over a virtual female avatar. Their findings suggest that 1st PP and synchronous touch are important factors for inducing the illusion of body ownership in VEs [149]. Banakou et al. use a VR setup projected in HMD to show that when adults experience visual-motor synchrony between their physical body and an avatar's body, they can embody a virtual avatar of a four-year-old child and an adult scaled to the same height as the child [156]. The findings of Banakou et al. also showed that due to the embodiment the adults overestimated the actual size of objects [156]. The findings of the previous research provide evidence of the usefulness of VR in exploring the plasticity of body representation.

In VR participants can embody a self-avatar of different age or gender

3.1.3   *Assessing perception of own body size using indirect measures*

Humans' perception of their surrounding space is determined by the human's capabilities to perform actions and interact with the environment [157]. Therefore, any change in the human body is related with a change in the perception of the surrounding space [157]. The possibilities for actions that are defined by the relationship between the perceived spatial layout and the organism's ability to perform the action Gibson defined as affordances [157]. Thus the affordance judgments are estimations as to whether the environment affords an action considering the individual's action capabilities in relation to their perceived size. For instance, when someone intends to perform an action, such as passing through an aperture like a doorway, the way the action is performed is influenced by the person's perceptions of their affordances [158]. It has been shown that changes in the width and the size of the body can influence decisions and estimations about affordances [159, 160].

Changes in body size are related to changes in perceived action capabilities

To perform affordance judgments an individual should consider their action capabilities in relation to their perceived size

Affordance perception is typically measured by having individuals estimate their ability to perform in a specific environmental setting. For example, perception of affordances for aperture pass-ability is assessed by having individuals estimate whether they can pass through apertures of various widths. A wealth of research has shown that humans are extremely accurate in their perceptions of affordances, even when the action capabilities of their bodies

Affordances judgments can be used as an implicit measure to access perception of body size

change or are artificially modified [159, 160, 161]. For example, if one's body width increases, individuals are capable of quickly adjusting their judgments of whether they can pass through an aperture accordingly. In order to be able to pass through an aperture, people need a space at least as wide as their body [160]. Thus, the width of the aperture depends on the width of the body. For this reason, affordances judgments can be used as an implicit measure to indirectly access information about the person's perceived body size.

3.1.4   Traditional methods for assessing perception of own body size

Body image in terms of visual perception of own body size has been assessed in many experiments using a variety of body size measures (see [41] for an overview of the literature), such as figure rating scales [41, 162, 163], distorted photographs [82, 137], drawing one's body [164], behavior matching, and affordance measures [165] (see [166] for an overview). The results from the research show that the precision of one's own body size perception can vary due to many factors [41]. Some of the main factors are psychological condition, thoughts and ideas about ideal body size, exposure to media [82, 167], and body satisfaction [82].

Figure rating scales and distorted photographs are often used to assess perception of body size

Hashimoto and Iriki 2013 used distorted photographs of participants' own bodies to show that women estimate photographs distorted by 10% in width to be photographs of their current body size, but photographs distorted by 30% in width were estimated to belong to others. Other work finds that healthy individuals show large distortions in size and shape of their hand [138] as well as their body [168], suggesting that people perceive both their hand and body to be wider and shorter compared to their actual size. Mischner et al. 2013 showed that exposure to music videos can bias both the perceived and the ideal body size of healthy women. Likewise, a large contrast between the idealized body promoted by the popular media (TV, music videos) and the average woman's body size [82] contributes to lower self-esteem and negative self-perceived attractiveness in healthy women [82, 167]. The discrepancy between women's perceived and ideal body size has been used to detect body dissatisfaction and bulimic tendencies [169], because people with eating disorders do not veridically perceive their own body size [169, 170, 171] (see [166] for an overview). More specifically, anorexic patients tend to overestimate the size of their body [172], while obese patients underestimate both their own and the body size of others [170, 173]. Due to the distorted representation of their own body image, often these people cannot identify themselves with the image that they see in the mirror [174]. Therefore, scientists suggest that VR technologies can be used as a tool to provide additional sensory information which will help people suffering from eating disorders to update their mental representation about their own body [12, 73].

There are factors which influence the precision of perception of one's own body size

3.1.5 *Limitation of the traditional methods used for generating the visual stimuli used in body perception research*

Most studies assessing body perception have used optical techniques to manipulate body shape, such as distorted videos [175, 176], distorted mirrors
[177] or distorted photographs [137]. However, these methods usually apply
uniform width changes to the visually portrayed body geometry, and thus, result in unrealistic body deformations. While in reality gaining weight does not
result in uniform changes in body geometry, but rather in multi-dimensional
nonuniform changes. For this reason when measuring body size perception,
some researchers have used figure rating scales [41, 138, 162, 163] that considered shape changes and fat distribution. Still, it is often difficult for the individual to identify with a figure not depicting features specific to the person,
such as shape particularities, wrinkles, skin color, freckles, moles and more.
Each of these features may impact the precision of body perception. Further,
this might be a potential reason why several studies show that estimations of
the size of the whole body produce more accurate results than estimates of
separate body parts [169, 171].

The traditional methods used for generating the visual stimuli in body perception research often result in unrealistic body deformations

Most of the methods that have been used so far for generating the visual
stimuli of the body perception experiments provide limited options for manipulating visual cues, such as shape. Even though a large literature has examined the way visual cues (e.g. shape and texture) influence perception of
objects and the way shape from shading is involved in object perception (see
[178, 179]), fewer studies have looked at the influence of texture information
on human body perception.

Little is known about the influence of visual cues on body perception

Thompson and Mikellidou 2011 showed an effect of texture pattern (horizontal or vertical lines) on the perception of the body size of a pictured mannequin. The effect of the texture pattern is consistent with the Helmholtz visual illusion, in which the length of the vertical stripes need to be extended
vertically to match the perceived extent of the horizontal stripes, whereas horizontal stripes need to be increased in width to match the perceived length of
the vertical stripes. Their results are in direct opposition to the well known
fashion tip that clothes with horizontal patterns make you look fatter, but vertical stripes are slimming. To my knowledge, no study has yet investigated
both shape and texture information for the perception of human body image
possibly due to the difficulty in implementing these changes with optical techniques.

The influence of texture and shape on body perception has not yet been investigated

3.2 PERCEPTION OF SPACE AND VISUAL CUES IN IMMERSIVE DISPLAYS

In order to improve the realism of the virtual worlds and the usefulness of
VR technology, scientists have investigated the differences between the real
and the virtual world, with respect to the sensory information provided in the
virtual world, as well as with regard to the user's perception and action [14,
15, 17]. Most of the studies investigating space perception in VEs have been

Most of the space perception research in VR investigates perception in HMD VEs

LSIDs have rarely
been a topic of
research

conducted using HMDs. Interestingly, the estimation of egocentric distances in LSIDs has rarely been a topic of research, even though LSIDs are also commonly used setups for immersive VR [3].

3.2.1   Measuring egocentric distance perception in the real world and the VE

Estimation of egocentric distances is often used for providing information about space perception in both real and virtual worlds [18, 19, 20, 21, 22, 23,

Distance perception
is assessed using
action-based and
cognitive-based
response measures

24, 25, 26]. Egocentric distance perception has been assessed using action-based response measures, such as direct blind walking (walking blindfolded or with eyes closed to a previously viewed target) [20, 22, 30, 132, 181, 182, 183], triangulated blind walking (after being turned to the side walking blindfolded or with eyes closed the distance between the individual and a previously viewed target) [21, 83, 184], pointing and throwing to a previously viewed target [26], or using cognitive-based measures, i.e. verbal reports (oral subjective estimations about the distance to an observed target) [21, 183] or timed imagined walking (estimating the time it will take to reach a previously viewed target by starting a stopwatch when the individual imagines starting to walk and stopping the stopwatch when the individual imagines reaching the target, where the individual does not look at the stopwatch) [20, 21, 22].

In the real world
people veridically
judge egocentric
distances using
action-based
measures

Overall visual information specifying depth in the real world is sufficient for viewers to veridically judge egocentric distances using action-based measures [23, 181, 182, 185, 186]. Kuhl et al. 2006 analyzed of direct blind walking in the real world and found that on average people were able to walk, without vision, to previously seen targets up to 12m with 96% accuracy. Their research suggests that the variability of the performance of individuals in direct blind walking does not require a large number of participants, but cautioned that even without feedback people become more accurate at performing the task over time.

In the real world
people
cognitive-based
measures have been
slightly
underestimated

In contrast to action-based measures, the cognitive-based measures in the real world have been shown to be slightly underestimated (82% of the actual distance) [185]. The amount of underestimation is reported to be systematic over the distances and is likely due to an underestimation of the metric scale and not an underestimation of space perception [20, 24]. The variability of cognitive estimates of egocentric distances can be reduced by providing the viewer with an absolute distance scale, such as a foot or a meter [187]. Additionally, there are other factors that have been shown to impact distance judgments. For instance, the research of Witt et al. 2007 demonstrates that distance perception in the real world is influenced by the layout of the space beyond the viewed target. More specifically, individuals tend to slightly overestimate the distance between themselves and the target when the target was placed near the end of a hallway, while the distance estimates to a target placed far from the end of the hallway were underestimated [188].

The reasons underlying the underestimation of distance in the HMD VEs are not thoroughly known, even though the response measure [26], the feeling of presence [30], the FOV [25, 29, 189], the weight/inertia of the HMD [28] and the quality of the computer graphics [183, 184] have all been investigated as possible causes. Some of these findings indicate that certain factors have a different impact depending on the response measure. For instance, the quality of computer graphics (in terms of providing a rich VE containing realistic textures and materials) has no impact on direct blind walking but it does influence verbal reports of egocentric distances [183].

The reasons underlying the underestimation of distance in the HMD VEs are not thoroughly known

Still these research results do not thoroughly explain the underestimation of distances in HMD VEs. However, these findings suggest that the visual stimuli (spatial layout, target, own visual body, type of HMD) in combination with the response measure have an influence on egocentric distance estimates. Several ideas have been proposed to compensate for the underestimation of distances in HMD VEs. Kuhl et al. 2009 suggest that the viewer's space perception can be altered by increasing the geometrical FOV in order to immediately allow users to make accurate judgments of egocentric distances. Leyrer et al. 2015 propose a change in the virtual eye height for compensating the mismatch in space perception. The researches of Mohler et al. 2007 and Richardson & Waller 2005 on HMD VEs propose an adaptation phase in terms of adaptation task or feedback, that are known to improve the accuracy of distance estimations.

Adaptation tasks, feedback and altering eye height or geometric FOV are among the ideas proposed for minimizing the underestimation of distances in HMD VEs

3.2.2   Visual depth cues specific to LSIDs

Egocentric distance perception in LSID VEs can also be influenced by the depth information provided by the different specifications of the LSIDs, such as, the shape of the LSID surface, the display projection (in terms of resolution, stereoscopic projection, brightness) and the additional technical setups (interaction mechanism, motion capture systems). In this section I do not cover all the visual depth cues available in the VEs (for an overview of all known visual depth cues see [23, 45, 126, 191]). I only discuss the visual depth cues that are of specific interest to the technical design considerations of the LSIDs, namely motion parallax, binocular disparity, accommodation, blur and convergence.

Motion parallax is a cue to depth, associated with the continuous change of the optical flow of the viewer based on a change of his/her viewing point relative to objects [192] and thus provides relative depth information about the distance between the objects and the viewer with respect to each other [191, p.412]. For instance, near objects (perpendicular to the line of sight) appear to move faster than far objects when traveling at the same speed. As defined by Howard 2002, the distance between two objects is proportional to the extent of motion parallax between these two objects. In a LSID setup, motion parallax can be provided through head tracking and can be used to enhance depth perception of the virtual scene [45, p.300]. Depending on the specific task that the viewer should perform, motion parallax may or may not be used as a string visual cue to depth. For example, motion parallax is thought to be a useful visual cue for perception of shapes [193]. However

Motion parallax provides relative depth information about the distance between the objects and the viewer with respect to each other

there is some evidence that motion parallax is a weak cue when estimating egocentric distances [194].

Depth cues such as, accommodation, blur and convergence, can be provided through a LSID. A stereoscopically projected scene possesses all the visual cues that a non-stereoscopically projected scene has and additionally provides binocular disparity [129]. Binocular disparity specifies the difference between the object's relative position projected on the retinas of the two eyes [23]. However, the perception of stereoscopically projected scenes is more susceptible to incorrect viewing position compared to the perception of a 2D image [127, 129].

Binocular disparity specifies the difference between the object's relative position projected on the retinas of the two eyes

Accommodation and blur are focus cues

Additionally, the information obtained by convergence and incorrectly projected focus cues (blur and accommodation) in stereoscopic displays can also lead to mis-perception of depth [129, 195]. In the real world blur is consistent with the eye's focal distance. The blur is a signal of the depth variation in the scene [195]. Due to the changes of the pupil size, the object, in which the viewer is fixated on, appears sharp and the other objects which are before or beyond the focal distance appear blurred [195]. This change of the pupil size, which allows the eye to focus and obtain a sharp image of the object is accommodation [23]. Accommodation is very useful for obtaining depth information when combined with other cues [195]. Accommodation and convergence are closely related as convergence is associated with the focusing of the two eyes of the viewer on the same object [23]. Convergence is measured by the angle that is made by the optical axes of the eyes [23]. For instance, the combination of convergence and accommodation can be very effective at providing absolute depth information for near distances [23]. In the LSID, accommodation provides information about the distance between the viewer and the display on which the virtual world is projected, while the blur represents the constant distance between the object and the display [195]. Therefore, when viewing a stereoscopic display the perceived depth may not correspond to the distance between the viewer and the object, but rather between the viewer and the display [195]. This conflict in focus cues might have an impact on distance perception in the virtual world. Perhaps by varying the distance to the LSID one can achieve less mis-perception of spatial layout [195, 196]. All of these differences between depth cues provided in the real world and in display setups make it challenging to convey depth cues, such as focus cues and convergence, in a natural way in LSID VEs.

The blur specifies the depth variation in the scene, due to the changes of the pupil size

Convergence is associated with the focusing of the two eyes of the viewer on the same object

Accommodation in LSID VEs specifies the distance between the viewer and the display

Blur in LSID VEs represents the constant distance between the object and the display

3.2.3 *Egocentric distance perception in LSIDs*

LSIDs have not been investigated as much as HMDs, even though they provide the opportunity to the user to see their own physical body while viewing the VR. Plumert et al. 2005 compared distance perception of distances beyond 6*m* in the real world to a non-stereoscopic LSID VE, which had three walls (a front and two side walls). In their research Plumert et al. 2005 both the VE and real world were viewed binocularly and timed imagined walking was used as a response measure. Participants underestimated distances compared to the actual distance to the target in both the real and the virtual world, but they underestimated imagined time to walk more in the LSID VE [20]. Plumert et al. 2005 also found that the tested distances had a different impact on distance estimations in both the real and the virtual world. The research of Grechkin et al. 2010 also involves a series of experiments conducted in the real world, in a HMD and in a LSID that investigate perception of space in VEs. They used timed imagined walking or direct blind walking as response measures for judging distances ranging from 6 to 18m. Grechkin et al. 2010 found that photo-realistic images of real world environments does not enhance distance perception in LSIDs, while distances estimated in the LSIDs using a 3D replication of the real world scene were underestimated to a similar degree as in the HMD [22]. Interestingly, Riecke et al. 2009found that several different displays (including HMD, conventional monitor 24$inches$ and large screen display 50$inches$) do not have an impact on blind walking. Participants showed highly accurate results for all of the different displays [83]. Possible reasons for these accurate results could be that they kept a fixed head position and orientation of their participants at 1.1m and by varying the distance to the projection surface kept the FOV the same for all of the tested displays [83].

> Several scientists found underestimation of egocentric distances in LSID VEs [20, 21, 22], while other report veridical distance perception [83].

Klein et al. 2009 investigated egocentric distance perception in stereoscopic LSIDs providing also motion parallax [21] and compared perception of distances ranging from 2 to 15m, in a real world environment to a CAVE and a stereoscopic tiled display wall VE (with stereoscopic projection and motion parallax). Klein et al. 2009 did not compare the results from the stereoscopic LSID VEs to a display which did not provide stereoscopic projection or motion parallax. Klein et al. 2009 used timed imagined walking, verbal reports and triangulated blind walking as response measures. They found an underestimation of egocentric distances in the real world, and a greater underestimation of distances in both the CAVE and in the tiled display wall VE [21]. Their results showed a strong agreement between timed imagined walking and verbal reports throughout the tested environments [21], suggesting that verbal reports are a reliable response measure. The research of Klein et al. [21] also suggests that action-based response measures performed in small spaces are likely to result in underestimation of distances, due to insufficient space to perform .

> The research of Klein et al. 2009 suggests that verbal reports are a reliable response measure for perception of distances

To summarize researchers investigating egocentric distance perception in LSIDs have provided inconclusive results as to the way distances are perceived in LSIDs. Further investigation of this matter is necessary in order to provide conclusive results, especially because LSIDs may be more informative for investigating body or even space perception considering that the user of LSID VEs is able to see their physical body while viewing the VE.

4

MOTIVATION AND RESEARCH QUESTIONS

It is becoming increasingly important to understand how users perceive their physical body and their self-avatar, as well as the influence of the self-avatar on the perceived space in VR. In the current chapter I first discuss the need of this research motivated by the field of computer graphics, gaming, clinical VR and clothing industry. Then I list some research questions and discuss them considering both computer graphics and perception of body and space in VR.

4.1 MOTIVATION FROM COMPUTER GRAPHICS, GAMING, CLINICAL VR AND CLOTHING APPLICATIONS

Self-avatars are progressively used in computer graphics applications, clinical VR and gaming, as well as in body and space perception research in VR. Therefore, it is beneficial to get more insights about the perception of the self-avatar and the user's own body, as well as how much should the avatar resemble the user in order for the user to identify with the self-avatar. Better understanding of these issues could make the experience of using VR technology for gaming and other VR entertainment tools more enjoyable and engaging.

Understanding the influence of the self-avatar on the user's perception could be useful for improving the realism of VR applications

Clinical VR will also benefit from the findings of this research and use them to develop VR therapies and diagnostics applications to gain new insights on body perception of individuals suffering from body image disorders (e.g. eating disorders or stroke). Researchers (such as Riva et al. 2008) pointed out that a major issue with VR applications used for therapies is that the patients often do not identify themselves with their self-avatar (see Section 1.3.4). Understanding whether self-avatars can be used to indirectly assess perception of own body in healthy individuals could be used to inspire new strategies for assessing body perception in individuals that are sensitive about their own body weight, size and dimensions (see Section 9.1 for more specific implications). Due to the conditions of such individuals it is often not trivial to generate their personalized self-avatars from 3D scans. Providing new insights on the range of weights that individuals accept as their current weight and the sensitivity to deviations from the individual's weight, dimensions and shape or the influence of visual cues on body perception, will be useful for clinical VR. Thus, the developers of such VR applications will be able to make important design decisions related to the specifications of the self-avatars (see Section 9.1 for more specific implications).

New insights about the influence of the self-avatars on perception could be used to inspire new strategies for assessing body perception in clinical VR tools

Another field that could use the findings of a research that investigates perception of one's own body and self-avatars is the clothing industry. On the one hand designers could use personalized self-avatars to design cloths.

On the other hand shopping is often time consuming mainly because of the queues in front of the fitting room. Therefore, some clothing companies use 3D scanners to scan their customers to provide them with faster alternative of the fitting room and also help them choose cloths that would fit them best [197]. Another field that could use the findings of a research that investigates perception of one's own body and self-avatars is the clothing industry. On the one hand designers could use personalized self-avatars to design cloths. On the other hand shopping is often time consuming mainly because of the queues in front of the fitting room. Therefore, some clothing companies use 3D scanners to scan their customers to provide them with faster alternative of the fitting room and also help them choose cloths that would fit them best [197].

4.2   HOW TO DESIGN LSID VR SYSTEMS TO PROVIDE THE USER WITH A REALISTIC EXPERIENCE?

Understanding space perception of LSID VEs beneficial for designing the spatial layout of VEs and improving the user's experience

Even though LSIDs are often used in perception research, the design of prototypes and visualization, so far many researchers investigated space perception only considering HMD VEs (see Section 3.2). The existing literature does not provide conclusive results as to whether the spatial layout of the LSID VE is perceived more veridical as compared to HMD VEs. In LSID VEs some visual depth cues (see Section 3.2.2) are perceived differently as compared to reality (see Section 3.2.2). More extensive research on the influence and the interaction of visual cues, such as stereoscopic cues and motion parallax in LSID VEs, will provide useful insights not only for researchers investigating space perception but also for programmers designing VEs for VR applications in LSIDs. The programmers and the designers of VEs, as well as body and space perception researchers can use the results for designing the VR setup and the spatial layout, as well as to improve the VR experience of the user (see Section 9.1 for more specific implications).

4.3   COULD VR USERS EXPERIENCE OWNERSHIP OVER A CONSIDERABLY DIFFERENT SELF-AVATAR?

New strategies and response measures for clinical VR tools that use avatars with a considerably different self-avatar than the participant

VR is an impressive and powerful tool to manipulate aspects of the body size and shape [78, 79, 81] or even the size and the distance to objects [151, 156] (see Section 3.1.2). All these findings suggest that the perception of the individual's own body can be manipulated in VR setups. Understanding the conditions necessary for embodying a self-avatar with a considerably different body size will have great contribution for increasing the effectiveness of VR applications. Furthermore, this research will provide new insights about the usefulness of VR as a medium to influence perception of own body size and the surrounding virtual world. Additionally, finding a new response measure, which is more reliable than subjective self-reports will be beneficial for gaining a better understanding of the mechanisms underlying body ownership (see Section 3.1.2). The outcome of this research will have implications especially beneficial for establishing strategies for developing new clinical VR tools for patients with body image disorders and especially, for VR applications that use avatars that do not resemble the participant (see Section 9.3.2 for implications).

Often when first exposed to the IVE people see a self-avatar, which is supposed to represent them in the VE, but they neither identify with nor embody yet. Therefore, I take a new approach on investigating embodiment by using a novel methodology to get a better understanding of which cues (e.g. visual, proprioceptive, memory, or a combination thereof) influence the participants' body perception, how these cues interact and to what extent each of these cues affects the participants' body perception (see Chapter 5). This approach could be of great interest for researchers investigating embodiment in VR.

This research introduces a new methodological aspect of special interest to researchers investigating RHI paradigm in VR

4.4 HOW PRECISE ARE PEOPLE WHEN ESTIMATING THE WEIGHT OF THEIR PERSONALIZED SELF-AVATAR? WHAT IS THE CONTRIBUTION OF VISUAL CUES TO THE PERCEPTION OF OWN BODY WEIGHT?

Most of the methods for generating the visual stimuli in the body perception research only distort the body in one dimension or use figures that do not portray individual specific features (e.g. [82, 137]). Interestingly, there has been a lot of research on the influence of visual cues, like shape and texture, on perception of size of objects [179]. However, little has been investigated in human bodies. The existing research on body perception and self-avatar perception in VR does not provide detail on how much the size of the self-avatar can deviate from the user in order to still be perceived as the user's current weight. Nor does it provide conclusive insights on whether the size of the personalized self-avatars is perceived veridical in terms of weight and whether people are able to veridically estimate their current body weight on a different body shape (e.g. stylized avatar or average personalized avatar).

Veridical perception of the self-avatar is desired in many VR applications, still the influence of visual cues on body perception in VR has not been investigated

There are many VR applications (e.g. VR medical diagnostics [85], ergonomics of seat belts [198]) or virtual clothing applications (e.g. [199]) for which not only the body morphology of the self-avatar's should be as similar as possible to the user's but also the self-avatar should be veridically perceived in terms of size. Therefore, it is important to investigate how much should the body of the self-avatar resemble the participant in order to be perceived as the participant's current body weight and whether people veridically perceive their own body weight as portrayed on their personalized self-avatars. Specifically, I investigate the influence of visual cues to provide new information related to the quality of the texture and the shape of the personalized self-avatar required for veridical perception of own body weight.

5

OWNING AN OVERWEIGHT OR UNDERWEIGHT BODY

Considering previous research, I investigated whether women can experience ownership over a virtual body that is considerably smaller or larger than their physical body, when viewed from 1st PP (see Figure 9). To gain a better understanding of the mechanisms underlying body ownership, I used an embodiment questionnaire. I also introduced two new behavioral response measures for estimating body ownership: an affordance estimation task (indirect measure of body size) and a body size estimation task (direct measure of body size). My aim was to find out whether these two measures can be used as reliable measures for body ownership.

I investigate the conditions required for embodying a self-avatar and introduce novel measures to assess embodiment of a virtual avatar.

Another novel aspect of this research, not found in the existing literature, is that I distinguished between the *physical*, the *experienced* (note, *experienced* body is a term which I use only in the paper for marking a distinction; the term was not used in any communication with the participants) and the *virtual* body:

THE *experienced* BODY - the body that the participant feels she has at that moment

THE *physical* BODY - the participant's own body

THE *virtual* BODY - the body that the participant sees when she looks down in the VE at the place where she expects her physical body to be

The aim of this threefold distinction is to offer a better understanding of which cues (e.g. visual, proprioceptive, memory, or a combination thereof) influence the participants' body perception. Additionally, the impact of these cues may vary between different setups, which is important for VR experiments investigating body ownership of a virtual body. For instance, in the VE presented on HMD the participants no longer have visual information about their own physical body. Instead, they receive visual information about a virtual body. However, they still receive somatosensory, proprioceptive and memory cues from their physical body. Thus, it is important to know how the cues that influence body perception interact and to what extent each of these cues affects the participants' body perception. The three bodies that I consider in this study tap into different cues that may influence body perception in VR.

The aim of the methodological novelty is to offer a better understanding of the contribution of various cues to embodiment and body perception

- the *experienced* body - a combination of visual, proprioceptive and memory cues

- the *physical* body - proprioceptive and memory cues

- the *virtual* body - visual cues

I predicted that after synchronous visual-tactile stimulation the participants would experience increased ownership over the virtual body. Thus, their reports about the *experienced* body would be biased by the size of the virtual body and they should experience a corresponding change in the perceived dimensions of their body. Additionally, I expected that, overall, body size estimations would be underestimated compared to the affordance estimations, because Warren and Whang, 1987, showed that in order for the gap to afford passing, the size of the aperture should be 1.3 times the size of their widest body parts. Therefore affordance estimations provide indirect measure of body size, in particular body width.

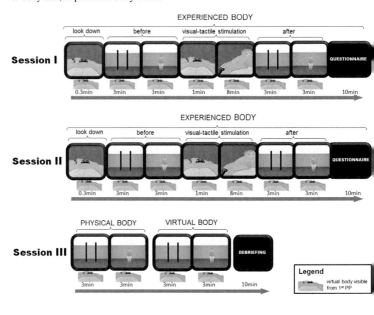

Figure 9: Schema illustrating the experimental design of the experiment that investigates the conditions required for embodying a self-avatar.

5.1 MATERIALS AND METHODS

5.1.1 *Ethics.*

The experiment was approved by the ethical committee of the Eberhard Karls University, Tübingen and written informed consent was obtained from all participants.

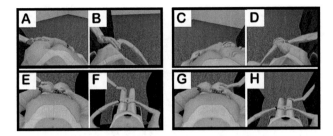

Figure 10: Perspective of the participant during visual-tactile stimulation. The animated virtual hand reaches through the black curtain to stroke the left arm (A - overweight, B - underweight), the right arm (C - overweight, D - underweight), the left leg (E - overweight, F - underweight) and the right leg (G - overweight, H - underweight) of the *virtual* body.

5.1.2 *Technical Setup.*

The participants' head motions were tracked using an optical motion tracking system described in Section 2.1.4.3. Thus, the participants received visual stimuli from a camera perspective that was updated to their head position and orientation (synchronous head motion), during the entire experiment including both the synchronous and the asynchronous stimulation. This was to prevent the participants from having motion-sickness due to asynchronous visual feedback [200].

The VR setup of this experiment uses an optical motion capture system, head tracking and HMD

The virtual scene was projected through nVisor SX111 described in Section 2.4.1. All participants were wearing the same HMD during the experiment, therefore any effect of the weight of the HMD on the participants' estimations should be the same for all participants in both the underweight and the overweight condition. The average end-to-end latency of the described network (i.e., motion capture system, processing the captured data, and streaming the processed data to update the scene projected in the HMD accordingly) was approximately $40.8ms$ $(SD = 24.0ms)$. The end-to-end latency was measured using photodiodes as proposed by Di Luca 2010. The participants used a Logitech joystick to perform the tasks during the experiment. The VR setup was implemented using Dassault Systemes 3DVIA Virtools 5.0.

5.1.3 *Visual Stimuli.*

The virtual scene included a virtual room, a chair, and a curtain behind the chair I modeled in Autodesk 3ds Max 2010. For the affordance measures I used the two poles ($0.2m$ diameter and $2.5m$ high) from Guess et al. 2010 (see Figure 12). The poles cast a bidirectional shadow on the floor of the virtual room. The poles were positioned at a distance of $3m$ from the participant.

The self-avatar was a modified under- or overweight mesh of a stylized female avatar from the Rocketbox Library HD

I modified a mesh of a stylized female avatar (from the Rocketbox Studios GmbH: Complete Characters Library HD) in Autodesk 3ds Max 2010 to cre-

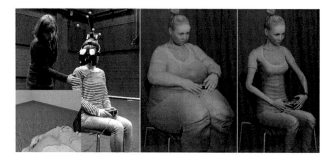

Figure 11: Left: The experimenter performing tactile stimulation to the upper arm of a participant wearing nVisor SX111, while the participant is viewing an animated virtual arm to perform the visual stimulation to the upper arm of the avatar shown from 1st PP). Middle: A screenshot of the overweight avatar used as visual stimuli for the experiment (Note the participants never saw their self-avatar from this perspective). Right: A screenshot of the underweight avatar used as visual stimuli for the experiment (Note the participants never saw their self-avatar from this perspective).

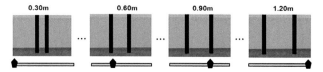

Figure 12: Affordance estimations: participants were able to smoothly adjust the width (from $0.3m$ to $1.2m$) of the gap between the poles. The pictures show the initial size of the gap in each of the four trials.

ate the meshes of the underweight and the overweight avatars (see Figure 10 and 11). The width of the hips and the shoulders of the underweight avatar were modified to be as thin as possible. Likewise I modified the mesh of the overweight avatar to be as wide as possible, but still human-like. The width of the hips and the shoulders of the stylized underweight avatar are comparable to those of a personalized female avatar with a body mass index (BMI) of 16. The width of the hips and the shoulders of the stylized overweight avatar are comparable to those of a personalized female avatar with a BMI of 43.

For each participant I adjusted the leg-, arm- and torso-length of the self-avatar (*virtual* body) to be same as these of the participant. During the entire experiment the *virtual* body was seated in the same posture as the participant, with legs together and torso straight, holding a joystick. Thus when looking down at the virtual scene the participants always saw the body of the underweight or the overweight avatar in the same posture as themselves. Note, that in order to track the participant's head motions in the setup the head of the *virtual* body was not visible. Thus the participants never saw the head of the

Static stylized self-avatar with the leg-, arm- and torso-length adjusted to these of the participant

1st PP *virtual* body, nor were they given any additional information about the head of the *virtual* body.

For the body size estimation task, the *virtual* body was shown from 3rd PP (3rd PP avatar) to the participants (see Figure 13). The 3rd PP avatar also had the same leg-, arm- and torso-length as the participant. Just like the poles in the affordance estimation task, the 3rd PP avatar was positioned $3m$ in front of the participants (see Figure 13). To enable smooth adjustment of the body size of the 3rd PP avatar I modified the meshes of the underweight and the overweight avatars to create blend shapes (a standard technique in computer animation for changing the shape of objects by interpolating between different meshes) in Autodesk 3ds Max 2010.

I used blend shapes for morphing to allow participants to smoothly adjust the avatar's body size in the body size estimation task

To provide the visual stimulation in the virtual scene I used an animated arm of a female character (from the Rocketbox Studios GmbH: Complete Characters Library HD) that was reaching out of a curtain and stroking the legs and arms of the participant (see Figure 10).

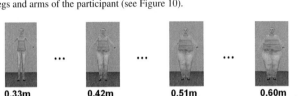

0.33m   0.42m   0.51m   0.60m

Figure 13: Body size estimations: the participants were able to smoothly adjust the size of the avatar, ranging in width from $0.33m$ (the underweight avatar) to $0.60m$ (the overweight avatar). The pictures show the initial size of the 3rd PP avatar in each of the four trials.

5.1.4 *Response measures.*

For each body type (*physical*, *experienced* and *virtual*) (session I, II and III) I used affordance and body size estimations as response measures (see Figure 12 and Figure 13). Additionally, for the *experienced* body (session I and II) I used an embodiment questionnaire probing the participants' sense of *ownership* (e.g. "...belongs to me"), *agency* (e.g. "I have control over...") and *location* (e.g. "I was sitting in the same location ...") (see Table 1). The categories were formed based on the literature and tailored to the specific experiment [142, 143, 144]. Even though it has been shown [145] that the illusion spreads over the whole body, I was not sure whether this would also be true for a *virtual* body of a considerably different size than the participant's body. This is why I included ownership and agency questions for each limb separately. The embodiment questionnaire consisted of 34 questions. For each session the questions were listed in randomized order for each participant. The questions used in this experiment are similar to questions used in other body ownership experiments [78, 81, 143, 144, 150, 203]. I used a Likert scale that

Affordance and body size estimations are used as response measures

The questions of the questionnaire refer to sense of ownership, agency and location - categories formed based on the literature

ranged from *fully disagree* (1) to *fully agree* (7). The middle anchor in the questionnaire scale was (4) but the participants were not explicitly told that this is the point of uncertainty.

5.1.5 *Participants.*

Thirty-two female participants with weight in the normal BMI range and no history of eating disorders

Thirty-two female participants (average age 26 years) with average BMI of 22.08, $SD = 2.95$, (average weight of $63kg$, $SD = 8.27kg$, average hip width - $0.37m$, average shoulder width - $0.39m$) with no history of eating or mental disorders voluntarily participated in the experiment (see Figure 14). The participants were screened for eating disorders in the written consent form of the experiment and with an Eating Attitudes Test[©] (EAT-26[©]). Each participant was compensated with 8 Euros per hour for their participation.

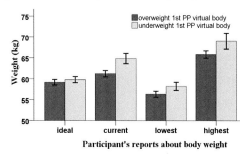

Figure 14: The graph shows the self-reports of the participants about their ideal, current, lowest and highest weight (since they were 18 years old). These reports were collected from the EAT-26[©] and used to screen the participants for eating disorders, in addition to the written consent. Error bars represent ±1 standard error of the mean.

5.1.6 *The Experimental Design*

Each participant participated in one of the two experimental conditions: under- and overweight self-avatar

All participants saw a *virtual* body from 1st PP, which was visible during the entire experiment. Half of the participants were randomly assigned to the underweight virtual body and the other half of the participants were assigned to the overweight *virtual* body (see Figure 10). The experiment consisted of three sessions (see Figure 9). The participants had five minute breaks between each session, during which the participant was not wearing the HMD.

Session I differed from session II only in the way the visual-tactile stimulation was provided (synchronous or asynchronous in a counter-balanced order). In both session I and II each participant was instructed to provide estimations for the body she feels she has at the moment (the *experienced* body). In the beginning of session I and II each participant did four trials of affordance estimations followed by four trials of body size estimations. The participant then

Table 1: The list of the items used for the questionnaire in the experiment and its scoring scale.

Sometimes ...

... I felt as if the virtual body was my body. (ownership)

... I experienced the virtual body as my body. (ownership)

... I had the feeling that I was looking at myself. (ownership)

... during the experiment I felt heavier than usual. (ownership)

... I experienced the arms of virtual body as parts of myself. (ownership)

... I experienced the legs of virtual body as parts of myself. (ownership)

... I had the feeling that I had a strong connection with the virtual body. (ownership)

... I was not aware that my physical body was different than the virtual body. (ownership)

... it felt as if I had more than one body. (ownership)

... I felt myself somehow connected to the virtual body. (ownership)

... I experienced the virtual body as myself. (ownership)

... it felt like my physical body was changing to take on the shape of the virtual body. (ownership)

... during the experiment I experienced my body bigger than usual. (ownership)

... I had the feeling that the virtual body belonged to me. (ownership)

... during the experiment I felt my physical body had become bigger. (ownership)

... it felt as if the body of the virtual body was my body. (ownership)

... I had the feeling that I and the virtual body were the same. (ownership)

... I had the sensation as if I was feeling the touch at the location at which the left virtual leg was stroked. (location)

... I had the sensation as if I was feeling the touch at the location at which the right virtual leg was stroked. (location)

... it felt like I was feeling touch at the same time as the virtual body was touched. (location)

... it felt as if the touch I was feeling was located somewhere between my physical body and the virtual body. (location)

... I had the feeling that the arm I saw was directly touching me. (location)

... I had the sensation as if I was feeling the touch at the location at which the right virtual arm was stroked. (location)

... I had the sensation as if I was feeling the touch at the location at which the left virtual arm was stroked. (location)

... I had the sensation as though the touch I felt was caused by the arm touching the virtual body. (location)

... I had the feeling that the touch I felt was caused by the arm I saw. (location)

... I had the feeling that I was sitting in the same location as virtual body. (location)

... I felt as if I was inside the virtual body. (location)

... I felt I could move the left arm of the virtual body if I wanted to. (agency)

... I felt I could move the right arm of the virtual body if I wanted to. (agency)

... I felt I could move the right leg of the virtual body if I wanted to. (agency)

... I felt I could move the left leg of the virtual body if I wanted to. (agency)

... I felt I could move the virtual body, if I wanted to. (agency)

... I had the feeling that I had control over the virtual body. (agency)

Requested answer for each item:

Fully disagree   O 1   O 2   O 3   O 4   O 5   O 6   O 7   fully agree

had one minute (exploration phase - see Table 2) in which she was encouraged to look down and around to get a good image of the body (the *virtual*

In session I and II (experienced body) the participants did body size and affordance estimations before and after visual-tactile stimulation (synchronous or asynchronous) followed by self-reports

body) and the scene. After that the participant received visual-tactile stimulation. The stimulation was provided for eight minutes in total - stroking both arms and legs for two minutes each, starting with the right upper-arm, then the left upper-arm, followed by the right leg and finally the left leg (see Figure 10 and Table 2). After the visual-tactile stimulation the participant did four trials of affordance estimations followed by four trials of body size estimations. At the end of the session, the participant took off the HMD and using paper and pen answered the embodiment questionnaire (see Table 1). The participants were instructed to give their answers to the questionnaire according to what they felt right after the stimulation.

In session III the participants judged the body size and the affordance of the physical and virtual body

Session III consisted of two parts. During the first part of session III each participant was instructed to ignore the visual information from the *virtual* body and to do four trials of affordance followed by four trials of body size estimations of her *physical* body. In the second part of session III each participant was asked to ignore the information (e.g. sensory, memory) that she perceives from her *physical* body and to perform four trials of affordance followed by four trials of body size estimations of the *virtual* body.

At the end of the experiment each participant was debriefed, filled in an EAT-26© in which they reported their current, their lowest and their highest weights and the experimenter measured the width of their hips and shoulders. In total, the experiment, including breaks between sessions, took about two hours.

5.1.7   Preparation for the experiment

The self-avatar was calibrated to the participant's height, arm- and leg-lengths

Before the beginning of the experiment each participant was given written and oral instructions by the experimenter. Then the participant's height, arm- and leg-lengths were measured for scaling both the *virtual* body and the 3rd PP avatar used for the body size estimation task. The participant then sat on a chair with her legs together and torso straight, holding a joystick in her hands. The participant put on the HMD and was asked to look down to report whether she sees a virtual joystick (the virtual joystick was positioned in the hands of the *virtual* body). Thus the participant's attention was indirectly pointed to the *virtual* body. This was to make sure that each participant saw the *virtual* body before performing the tasks.

5.1.8   Affordance estimation procedure

In the affordance estimation procedure the participants smoothly adjusted the aperture to allow the target body to pass through

The affordance estimation task consisted of four trials, in which the participant adjusted the distance between two poles to an aperture size that would allow the target body (*experienced*, *physical* or *virtual*) to pass through without twisting the shoulders or hips. The participants used a joystick to smoothly move the poles in either direction (step-size - 0.01m) (see Figure 12). The initial widths of the gap were 1.2m, 0.9m, 0.6m or 0.3m (see Figure 12). Each width was presented in one trial in randomized order.

5.1.9 *Body size estimation procedure*

The body size estimation task consisted of four trials, in which the participant used the joystick to adjust the body size of the 3rd PP avatar to match the target body (*experienced, physical* or *virtual*) (see Figure 13). Participants could smoothly adjust the body size of the 3rd PP avatar to the desired size/shape (step-size - 0.003m). For the body size estimation task I used as starting points variations of the 3rd PP avatar, in which the widest part was 0.3m, 0.4m, 0.5m or 0.6m (see Figure 13). Each was presented in one trial in randomized order.

In the body size estimation procedure the participants smoothly adjusted the body size of the 3rd PP avatar to match the target body

5.1.10 *Visual-tactile stimulation procedure*

The experimenter provided tactile stimulation by stroking (with her hand) the participant, either synchronously or asynchronously with the visual stimulation. During visual-tactile stimulation, the participants were asked to look at the direction of the limb that was being stimulated, and not to move their head (see Table 2). The experimenter made sure that the participant always had the limb in view by not starting the session until the participant was looking at the limb and by encouraging the participant to look at the limb being stroked at all times (see Table 2). Visual-tactile stimulation was provided through stroking for eight minutes in total - starting from the right upper-arm, then the left upper-arm, followed by the right leg and finally the left leg (see Figure 10). Visual stimulation was provided by a virtual arm coming out of the curtain. The experimenter provided tactile stimulation to the corresponding limb of the participant.

The tactile stimulation was provided by stroking in reality (the experimenter) and in VE (animated virtual arm)

5.2 RESULTS

5.2.1 *Analysis of the questionnaires*

I analyzed the answers from the categories (*ownership, agency* and *location*) of the embodiment questionnaire using Wilcoxon signed-rank tests with planned comparisons, because the responses from the ownership category in the synchronous session and the responses from the agency category in the asynchronous session from the overweight condition were not normally distributed, ($p = 0.031$ and $p = 0.004$ respectively). The homogeneity of variances was only violated for *ownership* for both the synchronous and the asynchronous stimulation, ($p = 0.016$ and $p = 0.022$ respectively), for the rest $ps > .01$. The analysis showed that significantly greater levels of embodiment were observed after the session with the synchronous compared to the asynchronous visual-tactile stimulation: ownership, ($z = -2.805, p = 0.005$), location, ($z = -4.919, p < 0.001$) and agency, ($z = -3.153, p = 0.002$) (see Figure 15). There was no significant difference between the levels of subjective ownership between the group that saw the underweight body and the group that saw the overweight body ($p > 0.05$).

The self-reports (ownership, agency and location) were significantly influenced by the synchronous stimulation for both the underweight and the overweight self-avatar

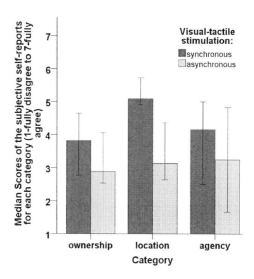

Figure 15: Graph showing the median score of the subjective self-reports organized into categories. Error bars represent 95% confidence intervals of the median.

5.2.2   *Analysis of the affordance and the body size estimations*

I analyzed the affordance and body size estimations to investigate whether the sense of body ownership over the *virtual* body (for both the underweight and the overweight) also had an influence on the participants' perceived body dimensions. Since I used a stylized avatar I could not precisely measure the BMI of each mesh. Therefore, I based the estimations on the widest body part of the participants and the *virtual* body. In this case this was either the width of the hips or the width of the shoulders. These are also the measurements that are most relevant for the affordance estimations. For analyzing the effect of the *virtual* body on the participant's perception, I calculated the ratio of the affordance estimations and the body size estimations based on the actual width of the participants. For calculating the width (both actual and estimated) I always considered the width of the widest body part (the hips or the shoulders):

$$\frac{estimation}{participant's\ actual\ width} = ratio \tag{1}$$

5.2.2.1 Affordance estimations

I performed a three-way mixed repeated measures ANOVA with the visual-tactile stimulation (synchronous vs. asynchronous) and the estimation (before vs. after) as within subject factors, the size of the 1st PP *virtual* body (underweight vs. overweight) as between subject factor, and the ratio of the affordance estimations (normally distributed - Shapiro-Wilk test $p > 0.05$, the homogeneity of variances was not violated after transformation $p > 0.05$) as a dependent variable (see Figure 16). The ANOVA showed a significant main effect of the size of the 1st PP *virtual* body (overweight - $M = 1.702$, $SE = 0.135$; underweight - $M = 1.265$, $SE = 0.068$) on the ratio of the affordance estimations, $(F(1,30) = 9.157, p = 0.005, \eta_p^2 = 0.234)$. The stimulation did not have an effect on the ratio of the affordance estimations, $(F(1,30) = 1.106, p = 0.301)$. The estimation (before vs. after) did not have an effect on the ratio of the affordance estimation, $(F(1,30) = 1.111, p = 0.300)$. There was no significant interaction between the visual-tactile stimulation and the size of the 1st PP virtual body (underweight vs. overweight), $(F(1,30) = 0.000, p = 0.990)$, nor an interaction between the size of the 1st PP virtual body and the estimation (before vs. after), $(F(1,30) = 3.661, p = 0.065)$.

The analysis showed a significant effect of the size of the self-avatar on the affordance estimations, but no effect of the stimulation

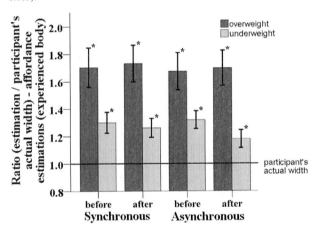

Figure 16: Plot of the ratio of the affordance estimations for the *experienced* body before and after synchronous and asynchronous visual-tactile stimulation. Error bars represent ± 1 standard error of the mean.

5.2.2.2 Body size estimations

The body size estimations for the *experienced* body were analyzed using a three-way mixed repeated measures ANOVA with visual-tactile stimulation (synchronous vs. asynchronous) and the order of estimation (before vs. after) as within subject factors, the size of the 1st PP virtual body (underweight vs. overweight) as a between subject factor and the ratio of body size estimations (normally distributed - Shapiro-Wilk test $p > 0.05$, the homogeneity of variances was not violated after transformation, $p > 0.05$) as a dependent variable (see Figure 17). The analysis showed a significant main effect of the size of the 1st PP virtual body (overweight - $M = 1.075$, $SE = 0.04$; underweight - $M = 0.926$, $SE = 0.021$) on the ratio of body size estimations, $(F(1,30) = 12.271, p = 0.001, \eta_p^2 = 0.290)$. The stimulation (synchronous vs. asynchronous) did not have a significant main effect on the ratio of body size estimations, $(F(1,30) = 0.353, p = 0.557)$. The order of estimation (before vs. after) did not have an effect on the ratio of the body size estimation, $(F(1,30) = 0.077, p = 0.783)$. There was no significant interaction between the visual-tactile stimulation and the size of the 1st PP virtual body (underweight vs. overweight), $(F(1,30) = 0.019, p = 0.891)$, nor an interaction between the size of the 1st PP virtual body and the estimation (before vs. after), $(F(1,30) = 3.331, p = 0.078)$.

The results indicated significant effect of the size of the self-avatar on the body size estimations, but no effect of the stimulation

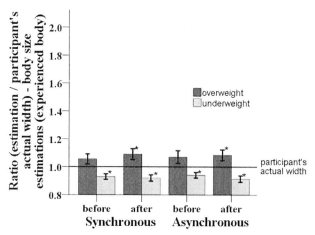

Figure 17: Plot of the ratio of body size estimations for the *experienced* body before and after synchronous and asynchronous visual-tactile stimulation. The asterisk (*) shows the estimations that are significantly different from the participant's actual width. Error bars represent ± 1 standard error of the mean.

5.2.2.3   *The effect of visual stimuli*

I further investigated whether the visual perception of the size of the 1st PP virtual body (underweight vs. overweight) had an effect on the estimations even before the visual-tactile stimulation. Using a paired-samples t-test I compared the ratio of the actual width (actual participant's width / actual participant's width = ratio of the actual width) to the ratio of the affordance or the body size estimation before the stimulation. The t-test showed that the affordance estimations for the *experienced* body were significantly underestimated (for the underweight 1st PP virtual body) and overestimated (for the overweight 1st PP virtual body) compared to the participant's actual width ($p < 0.001$) even before stimulation (see Figure 16). Interestingly, before the visual-tactile stimulation the body size estimations for the *experienced* body were significantly underestimated (for the underweight 1st PP virtual body: $p = 0.008$ - asynchronous; $p = 0.003$ - synchronous), but not significantly overestimated (for the overweight 1st PP virtual body: $p = 0.141$ - asynchronous; $p = 0.143$ - synchronous) compared to the participant's actual width (see Figure 17). Additionally, the head tracking data indicated that participants who saw the overweight 1st PP virtual body moved their heads less during the exploration phase and the visual-tactile stimulation as compared to participants who saw the underweight virtual body (see Table 2).

The analysis revealed an effect of the visual stimuli on the estimations of the experienced body estimations even before the stimulation

In the underweight condition - a significant effect on both affordances and body size

In the overweight condition - a significant effect on affordances and little effect on body size

Table 2: The average speed(m/s) with which the participants moved their head during the exploration phase and the visual-tactile stimulation.

Visual-tactile stimulation	Average head motion speed	
	Overweight avatar	Underweight avatar
No (exploration before synchronous)	0,010 3m/s	0,0154 m/s
No (exploration before asynchronous)	0,0120 m/s	0,0173 m/s
Right arm synchronous	0,0034 m/s	0,0035 m/s
Right arm asynchronous	0,0034 m/s	0,0036 m/s
Left arm synchronous	0,0037 m/s	0,0048 m/s
Left arm asynchronous	0,0035 m/s	0,0046 m/s
Right leg synchronous	0,0030 m/s	0,0036 m/s
Right leg asynchronous	0,0034 m/s	0,0036 m/s
Left leg synchronous	0,0032 m/s	0,0036 m/s
Left leg asynchronous	0,0034 m/s	0,0036 m/s

5.2.2.4 *Correlations*

I investigated the relationship of the mean values between the ratios of the subjective self-reports (*ownership*, *location* and *agency*) and the behavior measures (body size and affordance estimations) provided for each of the target bodies (*physical*, *experienced* and *virtual*), as well as the relationship between ratios of the participants' actual body size and the response measures (subjective self-reports, body size and affordance estimations). The analysis revealed several significant relationships between ratios of the subjective self-reports and the behavior measures in the overweight condition and in the underweight condition (see Table 3). Additionally, I found significant correlations between ratios of the actual size of the participants and the response

The results revealed several significant correlations, among which a significant relationship between the body size and the affordance estimations (see Table 3)

measures in the overweight condition and a significant correlation between the actual size of the participants and the body size estimations in the underweight condition (see Table 3).

5.2.3 Results - experienced body, physical body and virtual body

In contrast to sessions I and II, in session III participants did not receive visual-tactile stimulation (see Figure 9). In session III participants provided affordance and body size estimates about their *physical* body and their *virtual* body. The dependent measures for the *physical* body were obtained first, then the participants provided the measures for the *virtual* body.

Considering that in session I and II the visual-tactile stimulation did not have an effect on the affordance and body size estimations, I combined the estimations from session I and II. To gain more insight about the influence of the virtual body on the participants' perception of affordances and body size, I compared the estimations provided for the *experienced* body to the estimations provided for the *physical* body and the *virtual* body.

5.2.3.1 Affordance estimations

Body type (physical, experienced, virtual) had a significant effect on the affordance judgments

I performed a two-way mixed repeated measures ANOVA (and post hoc tests) with body type (*physical* vs. *experienced* vs. *virtual*) as a within subject factor, the size of the 1st PP virtual body (underweight vs. overweight) as a between subject factor, and the ratio of the affordance estimations as a dependent variable (the homogeneity of variances was not violated after transformation, $p > 0.05$) (see Equation 1 and Figure 18). The analysis revealed a significant main effect of the size of the 1st PP virtual body (underweight vs. overweight) on the ratio of the affordance estimations, $(F(1,30) = 16.588, p < 0.001, \eta_p^2 = 0.356)$. The body type (*physical* vs. *experienced* vs. *virtual*) had a significant main effect on the ratio of the affordance estimations $(F(2,60) = 7.119, p = 0.002, \eta_p^2 = 0.192)$. The analysis also showed a significant interaction between body type and the size of the 1st PP virtual body, $(F(2,60) = 38.516, p < 0.001, \eta_p^2 = 0.562)$.

For the underweight 1st PP virtual body the pairwise comparison using LSD adjustment for multiple comparison showed that at the .05 level of significance the ratio of the affordance estimates provided for the *virtual* body $(M = 1.043, SE = 0.046)$ was significantly underestimated compared to the ratio of the affordance estimates for the *experienced* body $(M = 1.265, SE = 0.064)$ (p = 0.001) and the *physical* body $(M = 1.297, SE = 0.061)$ $(p = 0.001)$. All the other comparisons were not significant.

For the overweight 1st PP virtual body the pairwise comparison using LSD adjustment for multiple comparison showed that at the .05 level of significance the ratio of the affordance estimates provided for the *physical* body $(M = 1.365, SE = 0.075)$ were significantly underestimated compared to the ratio of the affordance estimates for the *experienced* body $(M = 1.702, SE = 0.129)$ $(p = 0.001)$ and the *virtual* body $(M = 1.853, SE = 0.097)$ $(p < 0.001)$.

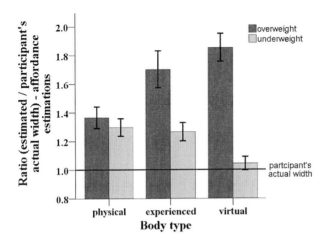

Figure 18: Plot of the ratio of the affordance estimates for the *physical*, *experienced* and *virtual* bodies. Error bars represent ± 1 standard error of the mean.

Additionally, I investigated the effect of the size of the 1st PP *virtual* body on the estimates for the *physical* body. Therefore, I performed a paired-samples t-test to compare the ratios of the affordance estimates for the *physical* body when visual sensory input of an underweight 1st PP *virtual* body was provided to when visual sensory input of an overweight 1st PP *virtual* body was provided. The t-test reveals that the ratio of the affordance estimates for the *physical* body are not statistically significant ($t(15) = 0.856, p = 0.406$).

5.2.3.2 *Body size estimations*

I performed a two-way mixed repeated measures ANOVA with the body (*physical* vs. *experienced* vs. *virtual*) as a within-subject factor, the size of the 1st PP *virtual* body (underweight vs. overweight) as a between-subject factor, and the ratio of the body size estimates as a dependent variable (the homogeneity of variances was not violated after transformation, $p > 0.05$) (see Equation 1 and Figure 19). The size of the 1st PP *virtual* body (underweight vs. overweight) had a significant main effect on the ratio of body size estimates, ($F(1,30) = 43.099, p < 0.001, \eta_p^2 = 0.590$). The analysis also revealed that the body type (*physical* vs. *experienced* vs. *virtual*) had a significant main effect on the ratio of the body size estimates, ($F(2,60) = 9.836, p < 0.001, \eta_p^2 = 0.247$). The interaction between the body type and the size of the 1st PP *virtual* body (underweight vs. overweight) was also significant, ($F(2,60) = 62.213, p < 0.001 \eta_p^2 = 0.675$).

For the underweight 1st PP *virtual* body the pairwise comparison using LSD adjustment for multiple comparison showed that at the .05 level of significance the ratio of the body size for the *physical* body ($M = 0.981, SE =$

Body type (physical, experienced, virtual) had a significant effect on body size judgments

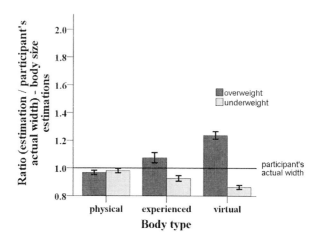

Figure 19: Plot of the ratio of the body size estimates for the *physical*, *experienced* and *virtual* bodies. Error bars represent ± 1 standard error of the mean.

0.015) was significantly overestimated compared to the *experienced* body ($M = 0.926, SE = 0.02$) ($p = 0.001$). The experienced body was significantly overestimated compared to the *virtual* body ($M = 0.863, SE = 0.014$) ($p = 0.001$). The *virtual* body was significantly underestimated compared to the *physical* body ($p < 0.001$).

For the overweight 1st PP *virtual* body the pairwise comparison using LSD adjustment for multiple comparison showed that at the .05 level of significance the ratio of the body size estimations for the *physical* body ($M = 0.968, SE = 0.015$) was significantly underestimated compared to the experienced body ($M = 1.075, SE = 0.038$) ($p = 0.005$). The experienced body was significantly underestimated compared to the *virtual* body ($M = 1.238, SE = 0.027$) ($p = 0.001$). The *physical* body was also significantly underestimated compared to the *virtual* body ($p < 0.001$).

Further, I investigated the effect of the size of the 1st PP *virtual* body on estimations of the *physical* body. I used a paired-samples t-test to compare the ratios of the body size estimates for the *physical* body from the underweight 1st PP *virtual* body to the ratio of the body size estimates for the *physical* body from the overweight 1st PP virtual body. The t-test showed that the body size estimates for the *physical* body are not statistically different ($t(15) = -0.674, p = 0.511$).

After session III the participants were asked whether and when they felt that the *virtual* body was representing them in the VE. Eight participants reported that they felt represented by the *virtual* body during both the sessions with synchronous and asynchronous stimulation. Seventeen participants felt represented by the 1st PP *virtual* body only during the session with synchronous stimulation, while the remaining seven participants answered that they did not feel represented by the *virtual* body (five - overweight 1st PP *virtual* body, two - underweight 1st PP *virtual* body).

5.3 DISCUSSION

5.3.1 *Discussion about the subjective self-reports*

The subjective self-reports indicated that after synchronous visual-tactile stimulation women experienced a significantly stronger sense of body ownership compared to after the asynchronous stimulation. The results are consistent with the findings from RHI paradigms employed in both the VR [78, 79, 80, 149, 151, 152] and the real world [139, 140, 141, 142, 150, 204]. interestingly, the participants are not completely rejecting the self-avatar after the asynchronous stimulation by providing responses around 3 for each of the three categories (*ownership*, *localization* and *agency*). This suggests that the synchronous head movements, the congruent visual perspective and the posture may have played a role in the illusion and were not negatively affected by the asynchronous visual-tactile feedback. Therefore, head motion and 1st PP may have partly overridden asynchronous touch. Unlike most experiments using a RHI paradigm, in my experiment the participants first estimated their affordances and body size, then answered the questionnaire. It is possible that for this reason participants gave lower scores for the questions than what they would report if the questionnaire were answered right after the stimulation.

Interestingly, the participants experienced not only a sense of ownership over the limbs of the self-avatar (underweight or overweight) which spread to the entire body (as found in Petkova et al. 2011), but also a sense of self-localization and a sense of agency. Probably, the sense of self-localization was induced due to the visual stimulus of the 1st PP virtual body. Note that in RHI paradigms employed in the real world the sense of agency can only be induced when in addition to the visual and the proprioceptive feedback, active synchronous sensory-motor feedback is provided [142, 144, 204]. My findings hint that in VR, the sense of agency can be induced without providing active synchronous sensory-motor feedback from the virtual body or its limbs. Furthermore, it seems that even though the head tracking was from the participants own head motions, participants interpreted cues from head tracking as if they were provoked by the head motions of the virtual body, therefore the participants felt a sense of agency over the self-avatar. Thus, the cues provided by head tracking were probably perceived as active synchronous sensory-motor feedback. This suggests that the illusion can even include the out of view head of the avatar. It is possible that the proprioceptive feedback from the participant's *physical* body and the cues provided by head tracking combined with the visual stimuli (1st PP virtual body in a similar posture) were enough to influence the participant's sense of agency over the virtual body. However, further research on this topic is necessary.

The self-reports are consistent with the related literature

Head motion and 1st PP may have partly overridden the asynchronous stimulation

The participants experienced sense of agency over the static self-avatar

The results hint that participants interpreted the head tracking as active synchronous sensory-motor feedback

5.3.2   Discussion about affordance and body size estimations

Both affordance and body size judgments are biased by the size of the self-avatar

I found that the size of the self-avatar (underweight vs. overweight) significantly biased the participants' affordance and body size estimations of the *experienced* body. Interestingly, the synchronous visual-tactile stimulation did not significantly impact the ratio of the participants' affordance and body size estimations. It is possible that the subjective self-reports and the behavioral measures (such as body size and affordance estimations) are influenced by different stimulation strategies. Therefore, in order to influence the affordance and body size estimations it might be preferable to use another type of stimulation or employ different methods for performing the behavioral measures.

Another potential explanation for why I found no significant effect of the stimulation on the behavioral measures is provided by the participants' reports collected before visual-tactile stimulation. Contrary to my expectations, the results showed that participants experienced a significant change in their *experienced* body size (only for the underweight) and affordances (for both) even before any type of visual-tactile stimulation. Considering the research of Normand et al. 2011 I think that the lack of effect of the stimulation on the body size estimations after the synchronous stimulation suggests that women might be more susceptible to visual stimulation and felt larger/smaller even before the tactile stimulation. However, further investigation is necessary in order to have conclusive results.

Subjective self-reports might be influenced by different stimulation strategies than behavioral measures

The results from the body size and affordance estimations tasks confirm the findings of Preston et al. 2014 about perceived body size when experiencing illusory ownership over a large body. However, I found no effect of stimulation for body size and affordance estimations tasks also for the thinner body. It is possible that the differences in the setup (e.g. VE, body size estimation procedure) caused the difference between my results and the findings reported in Preston et al. 2014 about the thin body.

Interestingly, the results from body size estimations relate to recent research of Hashimoto and Iriki 2013, which do not apply a RHI paradigm. Considering the related literature which employs the RHI paradigm, it is unlikely that the participants experienced full body ownership over the self-avatar only after looking at it for $0.3min$ without experiencing any type of synchronous visual-tactile or sensory-motor stimulation. However, it is possible that in order to influence the participant's body size and affordance estimations it is not necessary to use all the cues (e.g. a congruent position of the rubber hand with the participant's real hand [141, 148], visual-tactile stimulation [78, 79, 80, 141, 142, 143, 144, 148, 149, 150, 151, 152, 204]) necessary for inducing body ownership.

The combination of several congruent cues was sufficient to influence participants' perception of affordances and body size

The findings suggest that a combination of several congruent cues was enough to influence participants' perception of affordances and body size even before any visual-tactile stimulation. These cues, namely cues perceived from head tracking, visual cues (the underweight/overweight virtual body, which was viewed from 1st PP sitting in the same posture as the participant) and somatosensory stimulation (provided from the participant's *physical* body, which they were instructed not to move) were enough to influence participants' perception of body size (only for the underweight condition) and affordances. Perhaps another crucial factor for the effect of the *virtual* body on the *experienced* body size and affordance estimations was the method I used for conducting the affordances and the body size estimations. However, participants provided self-reports only after the visual-tactile stimulation, therefore I have no evidence for whether (in addition to the experienced change in body size and affordances) they experienced a sense of ownership over the 1st PP virtual body even before the visual-tactile stimulation.

5.3.3   *Distinction about the distinction between the physical, virtual and experienced body*

The distinction between the *physical*, *virtual* and *experienced* body that I made in this research is methodologically important for VR experiments (that employ the RHI paradigm), because it provides the ability to investigate specific cues that influence body perception. The three body types (*physical*, *experienced* and *virtual*) were perceived differently, as indicated by the affordance and body size estimations. Even though the 1st PP virtual body was visible during the entire experiment, the estimates for the *physical* body were veridical. Participants probably based their estimates for the *physical* body on their memory and the proprioceptive information they perceived from their *physical* body, and ignored the visual stimuli (as instructed).

The methodological novelty, namely the distinction between physical, virtual and experienced body, can be used to investigate the influence of specific cues on body perception

The affordance and body size estimates for the overweight 1st PP *virtual* body were significantly overestimated compared to the estimates for the underweight 1st PP virtual body. Interestingly, the findings suggest that in estimating the *experienced* body, participants integrated the information perceived from visual stimuli in the VE (e.g. the *virtual* body shown from 1st PP and head tracking) with the proprioceptive and somatosensory information from their *physical* body. Another potential reason might be that the participants were confused by the mismatch between the visual cues that they perceived from the VE and other cues, such as memory and proprioception.

5.4   SUMMARY OF THE MAIN FINDINGS

- Participants can embody a stylized self-avatar of considerably different size.

- Perception of body size can be influenced by showing a different sized avatar from 1st PP, in a similar posture and using head tracking

- Even before the visual-tactile stimulation participants experience a change in the perceived body size biased by the size of the stylized self-avatar

Table 3: The correlations between the ratios of the subjective self-reports, the behavioral response measures(body size and affordance estimations) and participants' measurements for both the underweight (u) and the overweight (o) conditions.

		Subjective self-reports (combined)			Affordance estimations			Body size estimations			Participants' measurement (width)		
		Owner-ship	Location	Agency	Physical body	Exper. body	Virtual body	Physical Body	Exper. body	Virtual body	Hips	Shoulders	Widest body part
Subjective self-reports (combined)	Owner-ship		u= .747**, o= .705**	u= .773*, o= .856**									
	Location	u= .747**, o= .705**		o= .603**									
	Agency	u= .773*, o= .856**	o= .603**		o=-.395*			o=-.445*		o=-.588**		o= .565**	o= .565**
Affordance estimations	Physical body			o=-.395*		u= .888**, o= .826**	u= .886**, o= .886**	o= .440*	u= .488*, o= .461*	u= .488*, o=-.427*			o=-.565**
	Exper. body				u= .888**, o= .826**		u= .529*, o= .835**		u= .529*, o=-.404*	u= .778**, o=-.404*			
	Virtual body				u= .886**, o= .886**	u= .529*, o= .835**		o=-.443*, o=-.445*	u= .521*, o= .456*	u= .521*, o=-.588**			
Body size estimations	Physical body			o=-.445*	o= .440*		o=-.443*, o=-.445*		u= .771**, o= .494**	o=-.494**			o=-.604**
	Exper. body				u= .488*, o= .461*	u= .529*, o=-.404*	u= .521*, o= .456*	u= .771**, o= .494**		u= .675**, o= .394*	o= .370*		
	Virtual body			o=-.588**	u= .488*, o=-.427*	u= .778**, o=-.404*	u= .521*, o=-.588**	o=-.494**	u= .675**, o= .394*		o= .465*	u=-.693**, o=-.829**	u=-.760**, o=-.829**
Participants' measurement (width)	Hips								o= .370*	o= .465*		o=-.604**	u= .712**
	Shoulders			o= .565**						u=-.693**, o=-.829**	o=-.604**		u= .880**, o= 1.000**
	Widest body part			o= .565**	o=-.565**			o=-.604**		u=-.760**, o=-.829**	u= .712**	u= .880**, o= 1.000**	

**p < 0.01 level, *p < 0.05 level, overweight (o) (N = 30), underweight (u) (N = 17)

6

SPACE PERCEPTION IN LSIDS

In this Chapter[1] I evaluate the precision of egocentric distance perception over a large range of distances in a series of experiments in both the real world and in three LSIDs with different specifications: a custom-made semi-spherical, a MPI CyberMotion Simulator cabin (MPI cabin) and a flat LSID. These LSIDs have commonly used technical setups, which are representative for display setups used in state-of-the-art VR laboratories.

6.1 MATERIALS AND METHODS

6.1.1 *Technical setup*

The semi-spherical LSID has the technical specifications described in Section 2.4.2 the participant viewed the VE from a distance of $3.5m$ from the front wall of the projection surface (see Figure 20). At the time when the experiment was conducted the MPI cabin LSID have not yet supported stereoscopic projection nor tracking of the participant's head position and orientation, therefore stereo cues and motion parallax were not provided (see additional specifications in Sections 2.4.2). The participants were seated as shown in Figure 21 (left).

The aim of this research is to evaluate the precision of egocentric distance perception over a large range of distances in three LSIDs: flat (head tracking and stereoscopic projection), cabin, semi-spherical

In the flat LSID the participants used shutter glasses to view the VE stereoscopically (the other specifications are described in Sections 2.4.2). In addition, a rigid object attached to the glasses was used to track the participant's head position and orientation. The shutter glasses have a horizontal FOV of $103°$ and vertical FOV of $62°$, which covers an area of about $2.1m \times 1m$ of the flat LSID, when viewed from a distance of $0.83m$ (Figure 22). This was the viewing distance in the each of the flat LSID conditions. Note that the difference between FOV of the shutter glasses and the flat LSID is only $2°$ horizontal and $26°$ vertical and the viewers were encouraged to look around and viewed the VE binocularly from their own eye-height (both physical and projected).

I consider that the technical specifications (i.e. shape and size) of the tested LSIDs differ from each other. For this reason I use the CoP as viewing location for each LSID and compare the distance estimations from each LSID to the distance estimations in the real world.

6.1.2 *Visual stimuli*

For the real world experiment I used a real room (dimensions $10.27m \times 7.25m \times 2.77m$) with tables, chairs, book cases, an air-conditioner, doors, win-

---

1 The candidate published this research in [205]

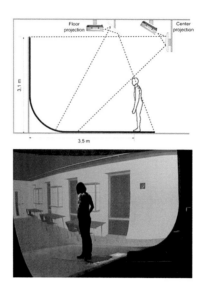

Figure 20: Top: The schematic image of the semi-spherical LSID. Bottom: A participant viewing the VE in the semi-spherical LSID.

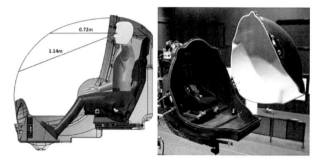

Figure 21: Left: The schematic image of the MPI cabin LSID. Right: The technical setup of the MPI cabin LSID.

I used a realistic replication of the real world environment for the LSID VE

dows and posters (see Figure 23). For all other experiments I modeled a 3D replication of the furnished real room that was modeled in Autodesk$^©$ 3ds Max 2009 with 10,488 polygons (see Figure 23). To make the 3D room more believable, the materials in the scene are as realistic as possible, created from photographs of the real room. Familiar size cues are provided through the content of the room, such as tables, chairs and book cases. For better real-time performance I used textures with repeating patterns. However, the texture gradients were created in a way that the user cannot notice any tiling of the carpet, the ceiling, etc. This was done to prevent the participants from using the tiled

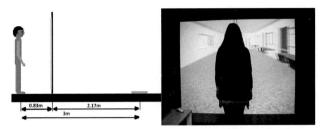

Figure 22: Left: The schematic image of the flat LSID. Right: A participant viewing
the stereoscopically projected VE in the flat LSID.

textures to make relative judgments (based on the tilings of the texture) between the different trials. I used global lighting in the 3D model. Therefore,
the lighting in the model was not as realistic as the lighting in the real world.
The 3D model was exported in Virtools 5.0 (3DVIA Dassault Systemes©).
This platform was also used for setting up the program for controlling the
experiment in the LSIDs.

6.1.3 Experimental design

The experiments had a between-subjects design. Altogether 77 participants
(35 male and 42 female), who had normal or corrected to normal vision, participated in the experiments. None of them saw the real room used for this
research before taking part in the experiment. Each participant took part in
only one condition (in only one of the experiments) and viewed the environment binocularly. Each participant viewed the environment from the same
location of the real/virtual room. In the semi-spherical LSID and in the MPI
cabin LSID the virtual room was not projected stereoscopically, while in the
flat LSID I varied the availability of stereoscopic projection and motion parallax, resulting in 4 conditions for the flat LSID. I used blind walking and
verbal reports of egocentric distances as response measures in the experiment
conducted in the real room. Due to the limited space to perform, in the LSID
experiments (the semi-spherical LSID, the MPI cabin LSID and the flat LSID)
I used only verbal reports as a response measure. The task of the participants
was to report as accurate as possible the distance between themselves and the
center of the target.

*Each participant
participated in one
condition: real world,
cabin LSID,
semi-spherical LSID
or one the flat LSID
conditions*

   Each experiment consisted of either 27 or 30 trials, containing 3 training
trials followed by the rest 24 or 27 trials respectively. The three training trials
were the same for all participants. They were used as a training phase to
assure that each participant understood the task. The following trials were
organized into 3 blocks in which each distance appeared only once per block
in a random order. For each trial a green target was placed on the floor of
the real or virtual room at different distances ranging from 1.5*m* to 6*m*. The
target used for the real world was an octagon made of green cardboard with

circumradius of 21.5*cm*. The target used for the VE conditions was a 3D green octagon with the same dimensions (see Figure 23).

Figure 23: Left: The room used for the real world condition. Middle: The 3D replication of the real room use for the conditions in the LSIDs. Right: A tilted view of the 3D replication of the real room with the green target on the floor.

The training trials were excluded from the analysis. Additionally, when comparing across the different locations, I excluded distances that were unique for the particular location (6*m* for the real room; 1.5*m* for the semi-spherical LSID VE), resulting in 8 distances per condition in each experiment.

6.1.4   *Experimental procedure*

For conducting this research I use the standard procedure for distance estimation experiments [39, 120, 183, 184]. Before the experiment, the experimenter tested the stereo vision of each participant using a 2D stereogram called Stereo Fly test from Precision Vision© (see precision-vision.com). Then the participant was given written and oral instructions for distance estimations consistent with Mohler et al.2006 and Alexandrova et al.2010. Finally, before beginning the experiment the experimenter showed the participant a stick, which is exactly 1*m* in length and has one division mark at 0.5*m*.

The experiments were conducted using a standard procedure for conducting distance perception experiments, similar to Mohler et al.2006 and Alexandrova et al.2010

During the experiment, while participants were viewing the real/virtual room they were not allowed to lean or bend about their waist, nor were they permitted to walk around. They were only permitted to move their head about their neck and were encouraged to take as much time as they needed to look around and get familiar with the environment. They had to give a verbal sign to the experimenter, when they thought they could imagine with eyes closed exactly, where the viewed target was located. After that they had to put on the blind fold (for the real world) or the experimenter blanked the screen (for the LSID VE). Then participants had to either walk to the place where they thought the center of the target was (for blind walking in the real world) or the participants had to turn their body or their head (in the case where they were seated) to the left and call out how far away from them the center of the target was located (for verbal reports). Forcing the participants to turn left for verbal reports prevents them from using the angle of their neck to compare the distance to the target between the different trials. Consequently the participants' judgments for the current distance to the target are not based on the judgment made for the target in the previously seen trial.

In order to start the next trial they had to turn back to their initial position. Then, they were permitted to see the real/virtual room again with the newly placed target. After the participants completed the experiment, they were asked to give the dimensions (in centimeters and meters) of the virtual space for the flat and the MPI cabin LSID experiments. In total, the experiment took about 90*min* for the real world condition because it consisted of two response measures, whereas for the rest of the conditions the experiment took about 30 − 45*min*.

6.2   EGOCENTRIC DISTANCE PERCEPTION IN THE REAL WORLD

In the real world 16 participants (6 male and 10 female; average age 27.9 years) saw the real room binocularly and had both verbal reports and blind walking, as a response measure for distance estimations. The order of the two response measures was counter balanced across participants to minimize order effects. The distances to the target for this condition were 2*m*, 2.5*m*, 3*m*, 3.5*m*, 4*m*, 4.5*m*, 5*m*, 5.5*m* and 6*m*. This experiment was used as a control experiment.

6.2.0.1   *Results*

Overall in the real world the participants estimated distances nearly veridically compared to the actual distances ($M = 95.77\%, SE = 2.944$). The distance estimations collected using blind walking ($M = 91.83\%, SE = 4.458$) are consistent with Kuhl et al. [182]. The verbal reports of egocentric distances of the participants are also on average accurate ($M = 101.11\%, SE = 0.614$). To further investigate the egocentric distance estimations I performed a two-way mixed repeated-measures analysis of variance (ANOVA) with distance and type of response measure as within subject factors, the order of the response measure as a between subject factor and the percent error of egocentric distance estimations as a dependent variable. The repeated-measures ANOVA showed a significant effect of distance to the target on the percent error of distance estimations, $F(8, 112) = 2.553, p = 0.014, \eta_p^2 = 0.154$, suggesting that the accuracy of the distance judgments is influenced by the distance between the target and the participant (see Figure 24). The analysis revealed no significant effect of type of response measure on the percent error of distance estimations, $F(1, 14) = 2.786, p = 0.117$, and no significant interaction between the distance to the target and the order of the response measure on the percent error of distance estimates, $F(8, 112) = 0.556, p = 0.812$. Additionally, the analysis showed significant interaction between the distance to the target and the type of response measure $F(8, 112) = 4.280, p < 0.001, \eta_p^2 = 0.234$. The interaction between the type of response measure and the order of the response measure was not significant, $F(1, 14) = 1.035, p = 0.326$, as well as the interaction between the distance to the target, the response measure and the order of the response measure, $F(8, 112) = 1.428, p = 0.192$.

The analysis revealed nearly veridical perception of distance is the real world

The accuracy of the distance estimations significantly depends on the distance to the target in the semi-spherical LSID

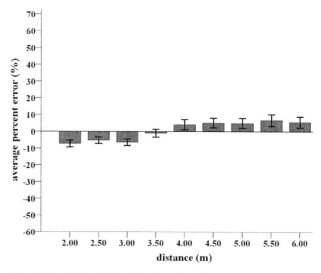

Figure 24: Plot of the results from the real world experiment per distance. Error bars represent ±1 standard error of the mean.

6.3   EGOCENTRIC DISTANCE PERCEPTION IN LARGE SCREEN IMMERSIVE DISPLAYS

6.3.1   *Semi-spherical large screen immersive display*

In the semi-spherical LSDI VE 11 participants (5 male and 6 female; average age 24 years) were standing at a distance of 3.5m from the front and the sides of the semi-spherical LSID and viewed the 3D model of the real room from a fixed eye-height of 1.7m. The floor of the VE was positioned to be on the same level as the floor of the semi-spherical LSID. The distances to the target for this experiment were 1.5, 2, 2.5, 3, 3.5, 4, 4.5, 5 and 5.5m. The 3D model was not stereoscopically projected. Motion parallax was also not provided.

6.3.1.1   *Results*

I found overall underestimation of distances in the semi-spherical LSID

Overall in the semi-spherical LSID VE the verbal estimations of egocentric distances were underestimated ($M = 83.17\%, SE = 5.21$) (see Figure 25). To determine whether the tested distances had an effect on distance estimates, I performed a one-way repeated measures ANOVA with the distance as a within subject factor and the percent error of verbal estimates of egocentric distances as a dependent variable. The results from the one-way repeated-measures ANOVA revealed a significant effect of distance on the percent error of verbal estimates of distances $F(7,70) = 109.259, p < 0.001, \eta_p^2 = 0.91$. More specifically, the participants significantly overestimated near distances up to $2m$, $t(10) = 3.359$, $p = 0.007$, veridically estimated the distance when the target was projected at $2.5m$ and $3m$, $t(10) = 1.908$, $p = 0.085$ and $t(10) = -1.311$, $p = 0.219$ respectively, and significantly underestimated the further distances beyond $3.5m$ ($t(10) = -5.305$, $p < 0.001$ for $3.5m$) (see Figure 25).

The percent error of the distance estimations significantly depends on the distance to the target in the semi-spherical LSID

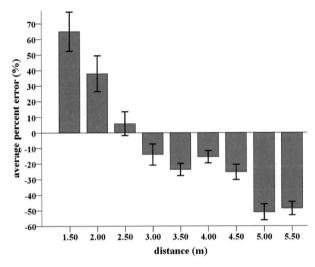

Figure 25: Plot of the results from the semi-spherical LSID experiment per distance. Error bars represent ± 1 standard error of the mean.

6.3.2 *MPI cabin large screen immersive display*

In the MPI cabin LSID 10 participants (9 male and 1 female; average age 33.4 years) were sitting at a distance of $1.14m$ from the projection surface and viewed the VE from a fixed eye-height of $0.9m$ (sitting eye-height). The floor of the VE was matched exactly to the floor of the MPI cabin LSID. The distances to the target were 2, 2.5, 3, 3.5, 4, 4.5, 5 and $5.5m$. The MPI cabin LSID does not yet support tracking of the participant's head position and orientation, therefore motion parallax was not provided. In addition, the VE was not projected stereoscopically.

6.3.2.1 *MPI cabin LSID Results*

The overall results show that compared to the actual distance the participants underestimated the tested distances in the MPI cabin LSID ($M = 69.64\%$, $SE = 5.37$). A one-way repeated measures ANOVA with distance as a within subject factor and percent error of verbal estimates of egocentric distances as a dependent variable, revealed a significant effect of distance on the percent

The percent error of the distance estimations significantly depends on the distance to the target in the cabin LSID

A significant
underestimation of
distances in the
cabin LSID

error, $F(7,63) = 9.29, p < 0.001, \eta_p^2 = 0.508$ (see Figure 26). The results indicated that all distances were significantly underestimated compared to the
actual distances. Even the least underestimated distance of $5.5m$ (see Figure 26) was significantly underestimated compared to the actual distance,
$t(9) = -6.961, p < 0.001$. For the MPI cabin LSID experiment participants
also estimated the width ($M = 60.179\%, SE = 10.249$), the height ($M =
111.05\%, SE = 8.204$) and the distance to the wall of the virtual room ($M =
82.26\%, SE = 6.989$) of the 3D replication of the real room.

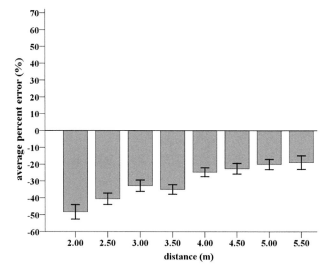

Figure 26: Overall percent error per distance in the MPI cabin LSID experiment. Error bars represent ± 1 standard error of the mean.

6.3.3   Flat large screen immersive display with stereoscopic projection and motion tracking

In the Flat LSID, there were 40 participants (15 male and 25 female; average age 27.8 years). The distances to the target were 2, 2.5, 3, 3.5, 4, 4.5, 5
and $5.5m$. The technical setup of the flat LSID supports stereoscopic projection and tracking of the participant's head position and orientation. Therefore,
motion parallax and stereoscopic projection were provided as two between
subject factors, resulting in four conditions (10 participants in each condition,
see Table 4) for this display type. Note that for the sake of legibility I use
'+', '−', 'S' and 'MP' to refer to the different conditions for the flat LSID
experiment, where '+' stands for available, '−' - for not available, 'S' - for
stereoscopic projection and 'MP' - for motion parallax (see Table 4) (-S-MP:

5 female and 5 male, -S+MP: 7 female and 3 male, +S+MP: 5 female and 5 male, +S-MP: 8 female and 2 male) .

Table 4: The conditions of the flat LSID experiment.

	Available motion parallax (+MP)	Not available motion parallax (-MP)
Available stereo (+S)	$+S+MP$	$+S-MP$
Not available stereo (-S)	$-S+MP$	$-S-MP$

All participants who took part in the flat LSID conditions had to wear NVIDIA$^{©}$ shutter glasses. The participants could compensate for the small difference in the FOV (see Section 6.1.1), especially because similarly to the rest of the experiments they were instructed and encouraged to look around and move their head during the experiment. The participants who took part in the +S-MP and +S+MP conditions needed the glasses, because the VE was projected stereoscopically. For rendering the VE scene in the +S-MP condition I used fixed disparity (parallel to the display). Therefore, the participants in the +S-MP condition perceived a correctly rendered stereoscopic image only when their eyes were parallel to the display and any other position or orientation of the eyes resulted in a slightly distorted image [207]. The participants in the other two conditions (-S-MP and -S+MP) wore the shutter glasses because I wanted to eliminate any between-subject effects in the flat LSID conditions.

In the flat LSID the availability of motion parallax and stereoscopic cues was manipulated resulting in four conditions (Table 4)

In the +S-MP and -S-MP conditions the head position and orientation of the participants were not tracked and the objects in the scene were stationary, and thus motion parallax cues were not provided. The participants in the -S+MP and +S+MP conditions perceived motion parallax cues through tracking of their head position and orientation, similar to the motion parallax cues provided in many distance judgments experiments conducted in HMDs [28, 30, 39, 120, 183]. Even though all objects in the scene were stationary, the participants were encouraged to use their own head motions to perceive motion parallax cues about the relative distance between the tables, the chairs, the windows in the scene by looking around the virtual world. They were encouraged to specifically look at the distance between themselves and the target. However, the participants were not given additional information such as the distance between two specific objects in the scene, which could help them use motion parallax also as an indirect source for absolute distance information. In both the real and the virtual world, the experimenter ensured that each participant was looking around the world as instructed.

6.3.3.1   Flat LSID Results

Overall the distance estimations reported by the participants in the flat LSID (see Figure 27) were underestimated ($M = 76.73\%, SE = 2.7$) compared to the actual distance. I analyzed the data using a three-way mixed repeated mea-

Overall underestimation of distances in the flat LSID

The percent error of the distance estimations significantly depends on the distance to the target in the flat LSID

sures ANOVA with distance as a within subject factor and motion parallax and stereoscopic projection as between subject factors and the percent error of verbal distance estimates as a dependent variable. The three-way mixed ANOVA revealed a significant effect of distance on the percent error of verbal distance estimates ($F(7,252) = 20,062, p < 0.001, \eta_p^2 = 0.358$), indicating that the percent error depends on the distance to the target. The ANOVA also showed no significant effect of motion parallax on the percent error of distance estimations ($F(1,36) = 0.472, p = 0.496$). Further, the three-way mixed ANOVA revealed no significant effect of the stereoscopic projection on the percent error of distance estimations ($F(1,36) = 0.003, p = 0.958$) and no significant interaction between stereoscopic projection and motion parallax on the percent error of distance estimations ($F(1,36) = 1.497, p = 0.229$).

The results showed no effect of motion parallax

The ANOVA showed also no significant interaction between distance and motion parallax on percent error ($F(7,252) = 0.881, p = 0.579$) and the interaction between distance, stereoscopic projection and motion parallax was also not significant ($F(7,252) = 1.080, p = 0.377$). However, the ANOVA showed a significant interaction between distance and stereoscopic projection on the percent error of distance estimates ($F(7,252) = 3.122, p = 0.004, \eta_p^2 = 0.08$) (see Figure 28).

A significant interaction between distance and stereoscopic projection on the percent error

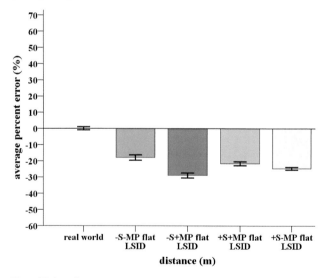

Figure 27: Overall percent error per condition in the flat LSID experiment compared with the real world. Error bars represent ±1 standard error of the mean distance estimation.

Since I used the Vicon system for tracking the participants' head position and orientation, I recorded the head position of each participant for every frame during the experiment. Using this data I calculated that the av-

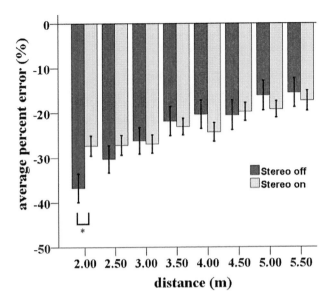

Figure 28: The plot illustrates the distance judgments per distance with and without stereoscopic projection. Error bars represent ±1 standard error of the mean distance estimation.

erage head motions of each participant during the experiment corresponds to $9.4m(SE = 0.96m)$ per minute. The participants that took part in the -S+MP and +S+MP conditions moved their head about $10.3m(SE = 1.38m)$ per minute on average, while the participants that took part in the -S-MP and +S-MP conditions moved their head slightly less, namely, $8.47m(SE = 1.34m)$ per minute on average. The ANOVA with the availability of motion parallax as a between subject factor and the head motions as a dependent variable, revealed no significant effect of difference on the head motions between the distance moved when motion parallax was present $(F(1,35) = 0.041, p = 0.84)$. Interestingly, the ANOVA with the availability of stereoscopic projection as a between subject factor and the head motions as a dependent variable, revealed a significant effect of difference on the head motions between the distance moved when stereoscopic projection was available $(F(1,35) = 4.439, p = 0.042, \eta_p^2 = 0.113)$

Further I observed the results and noticed that the data from the +S-MP condition did not seem to be greatly impacted by the distance to the target. Therefore I performed a one-way repeated measures ANOVA on the distance estimations reported in the +S-MP condition. The one-way repeated measures ANOVA with distance as a within subject factor and the percent error of verbal distance estimates as a dependent variable, revealed no significant

The analysis showed no significant effect of the head motions between the conditions with as compared to those without motion parallax cues

main effect of distance on the percent error of distance estimations when viewing was in stereoscopic projection only, $F(7,63) = 2.051, p = 0.062$. Similarly to the MPI cabin LSID, all participants in the flat LSID experiment were asked to estimate the width ($M = 77.71\%, SE = 3.95$), the height ($M = 133\%, SE = 11.25$) and the distance to the wall of the virtual room ($M = 88.55\%, SE = 3.59$) of the 3D replication of the real room (see Table 5).

Table 5: The dimensions of the room reported by the participants in the flat LSID VE.

	Dimensions of the room					
	Width		Height		Distance to the Wall	
Condition	Mean	SE	Mean	SE	Mean	SE
$-S-MP$	68.19%	8.2	113.10%	9.2	89.14%	6.75
$-S+MP$	67.23%	24.2	108.66%	8.77	68.88%	11.76
$+S+MP$	67.80%	14.78	119.18%	8.36	78.65%	14.58
$+S-MP$	70.25%	14.9	108.88%	9.85	81.71%	9.84

6.3.4 Overall Results

The relationship of distance to the target on distance estimations was evaluated using a linear regression analysis for each of the experimental conditions

The accuracy of egocentric distance estimation in the three LSIDs and in the real world were influenced by the viewing distance to the target (see Figure 29). In order to evaluate the relationship of distance to the target on distance estimations more precisely, I conducted a linear regression analysis for each of the experimental conditions (real world, semi-spherical LSID, MPI cabin LSID and flat LSID). The linear regression analysis was performed on the verbal estimates of egocentric distances with the actual distance used as a predictor variable and the mean error per distance as a dependent variable. The analysis of the results from the real world showed a significant linear relationship between the distance estimation and the actual distance ($F(1,127) = 14.36, p < 0.001$). The actual distance was able to explain 10.2% of the variation in the mean errors ($R = 0.320, R^2 = 0.102$). I also found significant linear relations between the actual distance and the mean error rate for both the MPI cabin LSID ($F(1,79) = 27.886, p < 0.001$) and the flat LSID ($F(1,319) = 21.44, p < 0.001$) experiments (see Table 6 for the slope and the intercept data). The analyses indicated that as the distance to the projected target increases in both the MPI cabin LSID and the flat LSID, the distance estimations become more accurate with respect to the actual distance. The analyses also showed that 26.3% of the variation of the percent error of the distance estimations per distance in the MPI cabin LSID can be explained by the distance to the target ($R = 0.513, R^2 = 0.263$), while only 6.3% of variation of the percent error of the distance estimations in the flat LSID can be explained by the distance to the target ($R = 0.251, R^2 = 0.063$).

As the distance to the projected target (in the cabin and the flat LSIDs) increases, the distance estimations become more accurate

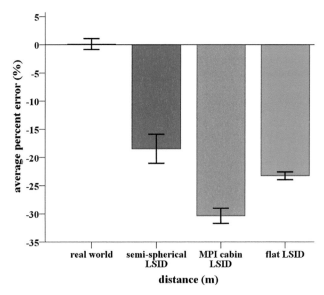

Figure 29: Overall percent error per experiment (error bars represent ±1 standard error of the mean).

Table 6: The dimensions of the room reported by the participants in the flat LSID VE.

	Real world	Cabin LSID	Flat LSID	Semi-spherical LSID
Intercept	-16.734	-61.627	-39.679	67.882
Slope	4.493	8.339	4.375	-22.59

For the semi-spherical LSID, the linear regression analysis revealed a significant linear relationship between the distance estimation and the actual distance $(F(1,87) = 106.9, p < 0.001)$ and explains 55.4% of the variation of the percent error of the distance estimations $(R = 0.744, R^2 = 0.554)$. The regression analysis also showed a negative correlation between the percent error of distance estimations and the actual distance $(r = -0.774, p < 0.001)$. However, a lack of fit test indicated significant deviations from linearity $(F(6,80) = 3.13, p = 0.008)$. The lowest order regression model which fit the semi-spherical LSID data is a cubic regression model. The analysis with a cubic model revealed a significant relationship between the distance estimation and the actual distance $(F(3,84) = 43.36, p < 0.001)$. The cubic regression analysis performed on the data indicated that 60.8% of the variance can be explained by the distance to the target $(R = 7.80, R^2 = 60.8)$.

Finally I was interested whether the effect of distance varies across the three LSIDs compared to the real world experiment (see Figure 30). I therefore examined which of the slopes and the intercepts of the regressions lines of the three LSIDs (semi-spherical LSID, MPI cabin LSID and flat LSID) were different from the real world experiment. To do so I built a regression model with distance, the LSIDs (semi-spherical LSID, MPI cabin LSID, flat LSID) and the interactions between the three LSIDs and distance (semi-spherical LSID*distance, MPI cabin LSID*distance, and flat LSID*distance) as predictors. Mean error rate was the dependent variable. Note, because I dummy coded the predictors of the display type, the three LSIDs are expressed relative to the real world condition.

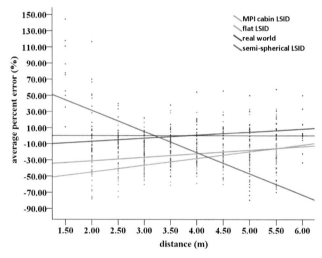

Figure 30: Distance effect patterns - plot of the linear regression lines.

Consequently, the three LSIDs predictors measure the difference of the intercept between the real world condition and the respective LSIDs experiment. Likewise, the interaction between the three LSIDs and distance measures the differences in slope between each of the display types and the real world condition. The results showed a significant effect of distance $t(1) = -3.08, p = 0.002$, a significant effect of MPI cabin LSID, $t(1) = -4.87, p < 0.001$, a significant effect of flat LSID, $t(1) = -3.39, p = 0.001$, and a significant effect of semi-spherical LSID, $t(1) = 9.45, p < 0.001$. These results indicate that the intercepts of all three LSIDs differed significantly from the real world experiment. As for the interactions, I found a non-significant interaction between MPI cabin LSID and distance, $t(1) = 1.64, p = 0.102$, a non-significant interaction between flat LSID and distance, $t(1) = -0.07, p = 0.945$, and a significant interaction between semi-spherical LSID and distance, $t(1) = -11.86, p < 0.001$. The first two non-significant interactions

The intercepts of all three LSIDs differed significantly from the real world

indicate that the slopes between the real world and MPI cabin LSID and between the real world and flat LSID are not significantly different. However,
the slopes of the semi-spherical LSID and the real world are significantly different. Hence, the results of this analysis suggest that the effect of distance
on the percent error for flat LSID and MPI cabin LSID is similar to the effect
of distance on the percent error in the real world experiment. The difference
in the percent error between the flat LSID and the MPI cabin LSID and the
real word consists mostly in a constant term that affects the percent error of
distance estimations in a similar manner across all distances.

*The slopes between
the real world and
MPI cabin LSID and
between the real
world and flat LSID
are not significantly
different*

6.4   DISCUSSION

The results from the three LSID VEs are consistent with other recent findings [20, 21, 22], indicating significant underestimation of distance perception compared to the actual distance, and in contradiction with Riecke et al.
[83], which is the only research that found no underestimation of egocentric
distances in LSIDs. The verbal estimates of egocentric distances provided in
the LSIDs were on average underestimated compared to the real world. Overall the verbal distance estimations reported in the semi-spherical LSID were
slightly less underestimated compared to the estimations performed in the
flat LSID. Likewise, the distance estimations reported in the flat LSID were
slightly less underestimated than the distance judgments in the MPI cabin
LSID.

*The underestimation
of distances found in
the three LSID VEs
is consistent with
other recent findings*

In the real world experiment the distance estimations performed using
blind walking are consistent with Kuhl et al. [182]. The verbal reports of
distances in the real world experiment indicated overall high accuracy. Interestingly, many researchers that investigated egocentric distance perception
using cognitive measures reported underestimation of distances, albeit by not
as much as in the virtual world [20, 21, 22, 24]. A major difference between
this experiment and previous research is that I used a meter as a scaling metric,
while all other experiments used feet. Additionally, I covered nine different
distances between 2 and 6m. Both of these factors could have contributed to
the overall higher accuracy of the verbal distance estimations.

I found a significant effect of distance to target on both verbal estimates
and blind-walking in both the real world and the LSID VEs. Even though
distances in the flat and in the MPI cabin LSIDs were significantly underestimated as compared to the real world, the same pattern of effect of distance on
the verbal estimations as in the real world is observed. Most of the previous
research, which investigated egocentric distance perception in both the real
and virtual world used only a few distances to evaluate distance perception
and therefore did not specifically focus on the influence of distance to the
target on distance estimates [24, 25, 27, 30, 83, 182, 184, 208]. Similarly to
Plumert et al. 2005 who studied distances beyond 6m, the results revealed
that the accuracy of the distance judgments in both the real and the virtual
world are influenced by the distance to the target. In the real world I found
a tendency of slight underestimation of near distances and slight overestima-

*There was a
significant effect of
distance to target on
both verbal estimates
and blind-walking*

tion of further distances. The research of Witt et al. 2007 might provide a potential reason for the observed distance effect in the real world. Namely, the slight overestimation of further distances could be caused by the close distance between the target and the back wall of the room. Since I used the same viewing location, target locations and a 3D replication of the real room, it is possible that the findings of Witt et al. 2007 might provide an explanation also for the distance effect found in the MPI cabin and the flat LSID.

Interestingly, the distance estimations performed in the semi-spherical LSID indicate an opposite trend to the distance effect as the one observed in the real world, the flat LSID and the MPI cabin LSID. The inconsistent distance effect in the semi-spherical display could be due to a combination of several factors, such as the shape of the LSID, the non-stereoscopic projection as well as the constantly changing position of the target with respect to the physical projection surface (floor, curve or wall). The combination of these factors may have led to conflicts in visual depth cues (i.e. blur, accommodation and convergence), to which the participants may not have easily adapted. As a consequence the conflict of depth cues resulted in overestimation of near (up to 2.5m) distances, veridical estimations for 3m and underestimation of further (beyond 3.5m) distances. Considering the findings from the flat LSID, that stereoscopic projection significantly impacts distances up to 2.5m, it is possible that stereoscopic projection might improve distance estimations for near distances in the semi-spherical LSID.

Conflicting visual depth cues could also be a reason underlying the overall underestimation of distance judgments in all of the three LSIDs. Probably for estimating the distances the participants accommodated their eyes on the projection surface and used a combination of other visual depth cues, such as familiar size, linear perspective or even blur, for estimating the distances. Familiar size and blur could provide also absolute distance information when appropriately combined with other cues. It is possible that for estimating distances the participants used the distance information provided from static visual depth cues (i.e. familiar size cues) in combination with focus cues (i.e. blur cues). In VEs blur cues provide information about the distance between the physical display and the target [195]. Therefore, the information, perceived from the visual depth cues provided by the LSID VEs, was not enough to result in veridical distance estimations.

I observed that providing only one of the factors (stereoscopic projection or motion parallax) impairs the accuracy of distance judgments, which is likely due to cue conflicts. The findings from the manipulation of the motion parallax in the flat LSID are supporting the results of Beall et al. 1995. I suggest that for an experimental setup and procedure similar to the one used in this experiments, motion parallax cues do not contribute to a greater accuracy in egocentric distance perception in LSID VEs. Probably when using other methods for manipulating motion parallax, motion parallax will have a greater impact on the accuracy of distance perception in VEs. For instance, if the participants were allowed to make larger head movements or I was using a pillars as a target on the floor, motion parallax would have stronger effect

The opposite effect of distance estimations in the semi-spherical LSID may be due to a conflict of visual depth cues

Possible cause of the underestimation in the LSIDs could be misperceived visual depth cues

Motion parallax did not have an effect on the estimations

and will enhance egocentric distance perception. However, further research on motion parallax is necessary for more conclusive results.

The findings from the flat LSID also indicated that stereoscopic projection significantly impacts distances up to 2.5m, but still there is an underestimation of distances. Even when providing both stereoscopic projection and motion parallax, the participants in the flat LSID significantly underestimated distances compared to the real world. Considering the research of Klein et al. 2009 which uses stereoscopic LSID (1.22m viewing distance) and the estimations reported in the flat LSID (0.83m viewing distance), I suggest that the distance between the participant and the projection surface plays an important role in egocentric distance perception in stereoscopic LSIDs.

Stereoscopic projection influenced perception of near distances

To gain more insights about the role of the viewing distance on distance perception, for future work, it would be beneficial to manipulate the viewing distance within one LSID. Further research on projection surfaces such as the semi-spherical LSID is also necessary, to determine whether the conflict of visual depth cues can be reduced. It would be beneficial to investigate the pattern of distance perception, when using only one of the projection surfaces (the front or the floor) of a LSID similar to the semi-spherical LSID. I also further propose that for improving the accuracy of distance judgments in LSIDs not only the magnitude of underestimation at a given location, but also the effect of distance for the given LSID should be determined. Further investigation on the cause of both the overall underestimation of distances in the LSID VE and the distance effect in the real and virtual world is necessary.

6.5   SUMMARY OF THE MAIN FINDINGS

- Verbal reports of egocentric distances are underestimated in all three LSID VEs, while distance perception is nearly veridical in the real world.

- I found an effect of distance to the target on the distance estimations in both real world and VE. The effect is not the same throughout LSID. Only the flat LSID and the cabin LSID showed similar effect of distance as the one found in the real world

- Stereoscopic projection impacts only near (2m) distance estimates

7

CAN I RECOGNIZE MY BODY'S WEIGHT? THE INFLUENCE OF SHAPE AND TEXTURE ON THE PERCEPTION OF SELF

In this Chapter I investigate the accuracy of women's perception of their own body weight. I explore this by altering the BMI of the participants' personalized avatars displayed on a LSID and additionally by manipulating two visual cues: shape and texture. I use a psychophysics procedure, a method of adjustment task and a similarity questionnaire to assess their perception of body weight.

The aim of this research is to investigate the range of weights accepted as similar to the current weight, as well as the influence of visual cues like shape and texture on body perception

7.1 METHOD

7.1.1 *Participants*

In my experiment, 13 female participants (see Table 7.1.1 for more information about range of BMI, weight, height, age, etc.) who had no history of eating disorders were compensated with 8 Euros per hour for their participation. Informed written consent was obtained prior to body capture and the experiment. Participants and the data were treated according to the Declaration of Helsinki. The recording methods of the database and the subsequent validation experiment were approved by the local ethics committee of the Eberhard Karls University of Tübingen.

7.1.2 *Generating virtual avatars based on 3d scan data*

The body scans from the participants were captured using the custom-made 3D full-body scanning system (3dMD, Atlanta, GA) at MPI for Intelligent Systems described in Section 2.1.2. Each participant was scanned in three poses (A-pose, T-pose and neutral) (see Figure 31 - second to the left). To generate the personalized avatars the collected scans were post-processed[1]

The personalized avatars were generated using 3D full-body scanning system

---

1 Since the candidate does not have direct access to the body model software, the research group of Prof. Dr. Michael Black and specifically Dr. Javier Romero post-processed the data from the 3D scans to generate the personalized avatars, as well as the personalized avatars with varying BMIs. The personalized avatars were generated by the research group of Prof. Dr. Michael Black, MPI for Intelligent Systems according to Hirshberg et al.[112], Bogo et. al. [113] and Weiss et al. [114]. In the remainder of this subsection I describe the avatar creation process as established by the research group of Prof. Dr. Michael Black. Since the candidate does not have direct access to the body model from MPI Intelligent Systems, the research group of Prof. Dr. Michael Black and particularly Dr. Javier Romero implemented (or provided) the algorithms described in this subsection to generate personalized avatars. Still, the decision related to the design of the personalized avatars and the design of the average avatars and avatars with varying BMI were predominantly made by the candidate.

	Range - Min.	Range - Max.	Mean
BMI	16.70	27.30	21.75 (SD = 2.92)
Height (m)	1.54	1.78	1.67 (SD = .06)
Current weight (kg)	49.00	74.00	60.68 (SD = 7.09)
Self-esteem *(15-25 normal range, smaller than 15 indicates lower self-esteem, greater than 25 indicates higher self-esteem)*	11.00	28.00	21.46(SD = 5.44)
Age (*years*)	20.00	37.00	27.38(SD = 4.48)
Self-reported ideal weight (kg)	45.00	67.00	57.69(SD = 6.14)
Self-reported lowest weight (kg)	48.00	65.00	54.23(SD = 5.83)
Self-reported highest weight (kg)	49.00	80.00	64.00(SD = 8.45)
Height/Weight distance (*see 7.2.3 for more information*)	5.91	0.16	1.29 (SD = 1.59)
Selected measurements distance (*see 7.2.3 for more information*)	3.54	15.94	7.72 (SD = 3.93)

Table 7: Descriptive statistics of the participants (N=13)

using a software developed by the research group of Prof. Dr. Michael Black, at MPI for Intelligent Systems.

First, during the post-processing 3D body model to the participants scan was registered. Through this process 3D meshes and textures that resembled the original 3D scans but that shared a common topology were obtained. This allowed to draw statistical conclusions from them. For the scan registration a statistical body model was used. The statistical body model compactly parametrizes body deformations in terms of deformations due to subjects' identity and body pose [112, 209]. Once registered, a texture map per scan after decomposing the colors observed in the RGB images into albedo and irradiance was extracted [113]. The final avatar texture map was computed as the median of each individual scan map.

The generated 3D meshes and textures resembled the original 3D scans but shared a common topology

The statistical body model is learned from registered 3D scans of nearly 2000 of different bodies in a single pose and thousands of 3D scans of many people in many different poses. From the registered scans of different people a low-dimensional statistical model of body shape variation in the population was learned. Following Anguelov et al.2005, the deformation of a triangulated template mesh was computed to every scan. Each triangle is described by a 3×3 deformation matrix that captures how the triangle has to deform to match the scan. An individual body shape is then characterized by a vector containing all the deformations that transform the template into the scan; this is a very high-dimensional description of body shape. To capture the correlated shape statistics in the population, these deformations for 2094 female

Figure 31: (From left to right) First - each participant's body geometry and image texture was captured using a 3D scanning system. Second - three poses (T-pose, A-pose and natural pose) were captured, resulting in high-resolution 3D meshes. Third - a statistical model of body shape and pose variation was fitted to the scans, bringing them into correspondence and using this model, a set of personalized avatars was created for each subject with varying BMIs (ranging from ±20% BMI change). Fourth - finally, women's sensitivity to changes in their perceived weight was accessed by asking them to estimate whether the size of the individual's personalized avatars displayed on a large-screen immersive display is the same as their current weight.

bodies in the CAESAR dataset were computed [210]. Then a principal component analysis was performed on the deformations and model body shape variation in a subspace, U, spanned by the first 300 principal components. This allows to compactly describe the shape of an individual, S_j, in terms of a vector of 300 linear coefficients, β_j, that approximate the shape deformations as $S_j = U_j \beta_j + \mu$, where μ is the mean shape deformation in the population. Here only female body shape was modeled.

To modify body shape, while keeping some anthropometric measurements fixed (i.e., height, arm length, inseam), it is necessary to model the relationship between identity deformation coefficients and relevant measurements. Similar to [114], the relation between identity deformations β and anthropometric measurements A was modeled as a linear mapping. Since it is linear, this mapping also models the relation between *changes* in shape coefficients and measurements, which will allow to modify β in a way that produces the intended measurement changes.

Mathematically, learning the linear relation between A and β corresponds to a least squares problem $(A|1)X = \beta$, where $A = [A_1 \ldots A_n]$ is a matrix of size $n \times m$ containing the $m = 4$ measurements of $n = 2094$ CAESAR bodies, $\beta = [\beta_1 \ldots \beta_n]$ is a matrix $n \times b$ containing the $b = 300$ identity deformation coefficients and X is a matrix $(m+1) \times b$ to be estimated. X describes the mapping between deformation coefficients β and the measurements $[w, h, a, i, b_0]$ (weight, height, arm length, inseam and deformation intercept). However, it also describes the relation between shape and measurement changes; for a given subject with shape coefficients β_i and measurements A_i (so that $A_i X = \beta_i$), changes in measurements Δ_A correspond to changes in deformation coefficients $\Delta_\beta = \Delta_A X$, since $(A_i + \Delta_A)X = \beta_i + (\Delta_A X)$. An example of these shape changes applied to an average body can be visualized in http://bodyvisualizer.com/ [94].

Given each subject's weight w, height h and 3D registration, the personalized avatars were constructed with nine varying BMIs $\left(1 + \frac{\Delta_{bmi}}{100}\right)\frac{w}{h^2}$, where $\Delta_{bmi} = \{0, \pm5, \pm10, \pm15, \pm20\}$. This was achieved by changing their identity deformation coefficients by $\Delta_\beta = \left[\frac{\Delta_{bmi}}{100}w, 0, 0, 0, 0\right] \cdot X$ (i.e., applying a change in weight equal to the desired proportional change in BMI, while keeping the rest of the measurements constant).

For each participant personalized avatars with nine varying BMI were generated

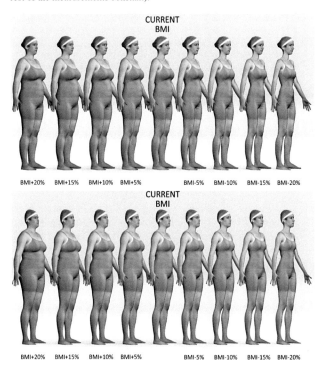

Figure 32: Top: An example of nine personalized avatars with varying BMIs generated given the person's weight (w), height (h) and 3D registration with the person's own photo-realistic texture. Bottom: An example of nine personalized avatars with varying BMIs generated given the person's weight (w), height (h) and the average female shape with the person's own photo-realistic texture.

Additionally, another avatar was created with same height h and weight w as the participant, but a different overall shape (e.g., different fat distribution, limb lengths, etc.) (Figure 32). To achieve this first the individual (with height and weight, h_{avg}, w_{avg}) in the CAESAR dataset whose shape and body morphology was closest to the average female shape was chosen. Then the height and weight of this individual's avatar was modified to match the nine varying

For each participant personalized average avatar and it's nine varying BMIs were generated

participant's BMIs previously computed by changing the deformation coefficients by $\Delta_\beta = \left[\frac{\Delta_{bmi}}{100}w + (w - w_{avg}), (h - h_{avg}), 0, 0, 0\right] \cdot X$.

Thus, the nine variations of the average body had different relative body proportions and shape than the participant's but the same height and BMI as the nine meshes generated from the participant's anthropomorphic data (see Figure 34). The texture mapping and mesh topology were the same for all meshes.

Figure 33: The checkerboard pattern texture used for texturing the personalized avatars.

7.1.3   Preparing the avatars for the interactive 3D visualization platform

After the personalized avatars were generated from the 3D scans, then I post-processed and prepared the avatars for the interactive 3D visualization platform that was used for the experiment. I post-processed the texture of the avatars of each participant to mask some black spots that were due to little data from the body scans or to due to not enough overlap between the texture of the avatar and the seems of the UVW map (see Figure 35) using Adobe Photoshop. I used a semi-transparent layer of Gaussian blur of 3 pixels to mask the entire texture but the region of the mouth, the nose and the eyes. Thus, while the individual's specific features we visible due to the original texture, their imperfections due to little scan data were masked with the semi-transparent blurred layer. Additionally, the texture was post-processed to match the color differences due to lighting (mainly brightness) between the participants' textures (Figure 35).

The texture of the personalized avatars were post-processed

In addition to the photo-realistic texture for the experiment a checkerboard texture was used for texturing both the own and the average avatars of different BMIs. The checkerboard texture was used because while removing some color- and texture-specific details of the avatar, it portrays shape information very well (Figure 33). The same UVW mapping was used for both textures through out all of the avatars. Therefore any effect of the UVW mapping on

A photo-realistic and a checkerboard texture were used for texturing the avatars

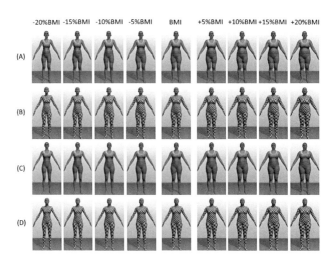

Figure 34: Picture with all meshes in the A-pose for an individual. Row (A) shows the set of visual stimuli representing an avatar with own photo-realistic texture and own shape. Row (B) shows the set of visual stimuli representing an avatar with checkerboard pattern texture and own shape. Row (C) show the set of visual stimuli representing an avatar with own photo-realistic texture and average shape. Row (D) shows the set of visual stimuli representing an avatar with checkerboard pattern texture and average shape. Notice for example that shape deformations in the avatar apply to all body parts in a non-uniform way as can be noticed in this 2D image in the ears, legs and the stomach area, especially when comparing the lowest BMI to the greatest BMI avatar.

the participants' estimations should be the same for all avatars (both those textured with photo-realistic texture and checkerboard texture).

For each participant, I combined the nine meshes generated from the 3D scan data in a morphable mesh in Autodesk 3ds Max. I also created a morphable mesh for the nine average meshes with varying BMIs. To prevent any differences between the generation of the morphable meshes I programmed a script which loads the meshes and assigns them as a target mesh to the mesh of the participant's current BMI. Then the participant's photo-realistic texture was directly applied to both the participant's shape meshes and the average shape meshes. Unity 3D was used for programming the experiment and setting the scene in which the mesh of the personalized and the average avatar with either texture were dynamically loaded.

A morphable mesh from the personalized avatars was generated for both the average and the own avatars

Figure 35: An example of photo-realistic texture after being post-processed in
Adobe Photoshop.

7.1.4 *Visual stimuli - virtual scene*

The visual stimuli were projected on a flat LSID (see Section 2.4.2). The
virtual scene included an empty virtual room with a personalized avatar. Prior
work has shown that there are orientation-dependent recognition effects in
object and shape perception [211], as well as face perception [212]. Recent
research also suggests that there may be orientation-dependent recognition
effects in the perception of body size [137]. Thus, the personalized avatar
was shown in a constant A-pose from a frontal view, as if the participant was
looking at herself in the mirror (a familiar and natural perspective) (Figure
34). The personalized avatar was placed at a distance of *2m* in front of the
participant.

Considering the research from Chapter 6 the personalized avatar was positioned at a distance of 2m in front of the participant

7.1.5 *Experimental design*

I measured participants' sensitivity to weight changes of their personalized
avatar's body (measured in terms of BMI) and manipulated the body's texture (own vs. checkerboard) and shape (own vs. average) in one interval with
2AFC and in a method of adjustment task. Specifically, participants' task in
the 2AFC part was to report whether the current presented avatar had the
same body weight as themselves. To this end the experiment had a 2 (visual
texture: own vs. checkerboard) ×2 (shape: own vs. average) ×9 (avatar BMI:
0%, ±5%, ±10%, ±15%, ±20% of current participant's BMI) completely
crossed, within-participants design (Figure 34 for example visual stimuli). In
the method of adjustment task the participants had to set the weight of the
avatar to match their current body weight. Additionally, the participants were
asked to adjust the weight of the avatar to match their ideal weight.

The experiment had 2 (visual texture: own vs. checkerboard) ×2 (shape: own vs. average) ×9 (avatar BMI: 0%, ±5%, ±10%, ±15%, ±20% of current participant's BMI) (within-participants) experimental design

7.1.6 *Experimental procedure*

At the very beginning of the experiment each participant had to fill out a self-esteem questionnaire [213]. The experiment consisted of four sessions. The order of the sessions was randomized. The presentation time of the visual stimuli for all tasks was not fixed and participants were instructed to make their estimates as accurately as possible. The only difference between the four sessions was the visual cues of the avatar (own shape with own texture / own shape with checkerboard texture / average shape with own texture / average shape with checkerboard texture) (Figure 36). Thus, in each session the participant was presented with only one set of the personalized avatars (e.g., one row of visual stimuli from Figure 34). More specifically, this was nine avatars with 0%, ±5%, ±10%, ±15%, ±20% of the current participant's BMI.

The experiment had four sessions: 1) own shape with own texture, 2) own shape with checkerboard texture, 3) average shape with own texture, and 4) average shape with checkerboard texture

TEXTURE RELATED CUES

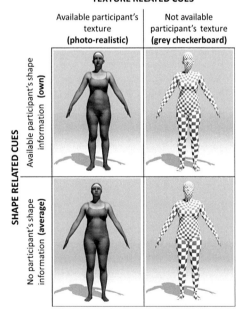

Figure 36: Schema using a personalized avatar of a person's current BMI to depict each of the four conditions according to the available visual cues (i.e. texture and shape).

In the 2AFC procedure participants reported: "Is it the same weight as you?(yes/no)"

Each session began with a 2AFC procedure where the participant had to answer "yes" or "no" to the following question: "Is it the same weight as you?" using joystick buttons. As soon as the participant pressed the "yes" or the "no" button, the screen went blank for two seconds. Then the participant was presented with the next trial. This procedure continued for a total of 180 trials. The trials were divided into 20 blocks, in which each of the nine stimuli (e.g., one row from Figure 34) was presented once. The order of the stimuli was always randomized. After 45 trials during the 2AFC procedure the participants had an opportunity to take a break if they needed it.

After the 2AFC procedure was complete, the participant performed a method of adjustment task, in which the participant had control over the intensity of the stimulus and her task was to adjust the weight of the avatar so that it matched her current weight. The method of adjustment task had nine trials and was programmed so that the values available for the range of the intensities of the visual stimulus were continuous (i.e., one unit of change corresponded to 0.05% BMI change). The starting point of each trial was one of the nine stimuli (in randomized order) presented in the 2AFC procedure.

Then, the participant performed another nine trials of the method of adjustment task (as described above), but this time the participant was asked to adjust the weight of the avatar to what she thinks is the weight which is ideal for her. After completing the method of adjustment task for the ideal weight, participants filled out a questionnaire in which they reported (using a Likert scale) the similarity between their body and the avatar that they estimated to be the same weight as their current weight, as well as general information about the way the avatar was perceived (e.g. How similar was the avatar to you? or How similar were the legs/arms/torso/face of the avatar to yours?). The participants were specifically instructed to answer questions according to the avatar that they estimated to be the same weight as them. At the end of each session the participant had a five minute break. At the very end of the experiment, participants were asked to complete a general questionnaire about their habits related to body perception and body weight (see Table 8).

After the 2AFC procedure the participants estimated in a method of adjustment task their current and ideal body weight, and reported the similarity between their avatar and themselves

Question	Answer
How much time (on average, per day) do you spend looking at your body in the mirror?	$M = 18.21$ minutes $(SD = 20.53)$
Do you often think about the way you look?	yes ($N = 7$), no ($N = 6$)
Do you often compare the way you look with the way other people look?	yes ($N = 9$), no ($N = 4$)
Do you check your appearance in a mirror whenever you can?	yes ($N = 5$), no ($N = 8$)
Do you usually notice even small changes in your weight?	yes ($N = 3$), no ($N = 10$)
Are you on a weight-loss diet?	yes ($N = 2$), no ($N = 11$)

Table 8: General questionnaire at the end of the experiment.

7.2   RESULTS

7.2.1   Sensitivity to own weight perception: difference for overweight vs. underweight

The analysis of the 2AFC indicated overall veridical perception of current weight

The mean proportion of the answer 'Is it the same weight as you?' is shown in Figure 37. Overall the participants estimated the weight of the avatar with BMI% change of 0%, regardless of texture or shape, to match their current weight. Yet, sensitivity to the avatars with ±5%, ±10%, ±15% and ±20% BMI change seemed to depend on whether the avatar increasingly became overweight (positive BMI% changes) or underweight (negative BMI% changes) as indicated by the fall-off rate of the mean proportion to both sides of the 0% BMI change point. In particular, the steeper fall-off rate for positive BMI% changes compared to negative BMI% changes suggests that participants were somewhat more sensitive to an overweight avatar than to an underweight avatar.

To statistically test these observed patterns in differences of the fall-off rate for positive compared to negative BMI% changes, a psychometric functions to the mean proportions of 'Is it the same weight as you?'-answers was fitted separately. Specifically, a cumulative Weibull function according to Wichmann and Hill 2001 was fitted. Alpha (position of the psychometric function along the x-axis, beta (the slope of the psychometric function), and lambda (the peak of the psychometric function) were free to vary. Gamma (flooring performance) was fixed to zero. The psychometric function was fit for each experimental condition and participant separately. The fit of the psychometric function to the mean data was good (mean $R^2 = 0.999$, $SE = 0.0004$).

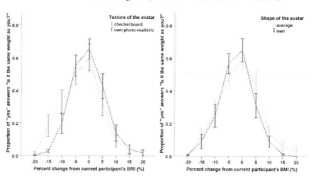

Figure 37: The mean proportion of the answer 'Is it the same weight as you' based on the dependent variables shape and texture and with varying amounts of BMI% change. Error bars represent ±1 standard error of the mean.

I examined the effect of shape and texture on lambda to examine whether manipulations of these visual cues affected the maximum proportion of 'Is it the same weight as you?'-answers (i.e., the height of the peak in Figure

38). A 2×2 within-subjects ANOVA showed no significant effect of shape (own vs. average), $F(1,10) = 0.11, p = 0.92$, or texture (own photo-realistic vs. checkerboard pattern), $F(1,10) = 0.432, p = 0.526$, and no interaction between shape and texture, $F(1,10) = 1.223, p = 0.295$ on lambda (the peak of the psychometric function). Hence, the maximum response was not influenced by the visual cue manipulations.

There was no effect of shape/texture on the slope

While there was little change with visual cues there was a clear difference in overall slope values depending on whether the presented avatar appeared underweight or overweight compared to the participant's perceived current weight (compare left and right panel of Figure 37). To better illustrate the difference in the fall-off, the slopes are shown for the texture, shape, and BMI% change direction (overweight vs. underweight changes) in Figure 38. Notice that higher slope values indicate greater sensitivity to BMI% changes. I examined the effect of texture, shape, and BMI% change direction on the slope of the psychometric function in a completely crossed within-subject ANOVA with texture (own photo-realistic vs. checkerboard pattern), shape (own vs. average), and BMI% change direction (underweight vs. overweight) as factors and slope as the dependent variable. Because the data differed from normality, I calculated the ANOVA on the power transformed slope values which restored normality. I found only a significant main effect of BMI% change direction, $F(1,10) = 17.28, p = 0.002$, indicating that the slope of the overweight direction was significantly steeper than the slope of the underweight direction. The other main effects of texture and shape and two- and three-way interactions between texture, shape, and BMI% change direction were all non-significant, $p > 0.05$.

The slope of the overweight direction was significantly steeper than the slope of the underweight direction

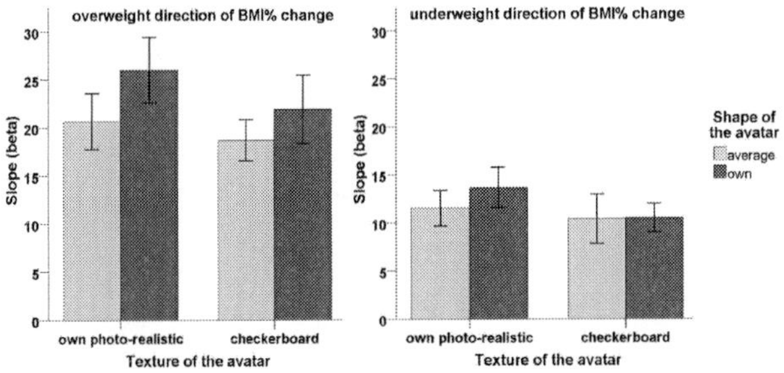

Figure 38: The effect of shape and texture on the slope of the psychometric function (beta). Error bars represent ± 1 standard error of the mean.

7.2.2 *The influence of shape (own vs. average) and texture (own photo-realistic vs. checkerboard pattern) on weight perception of avatars*

Are people able to estimate their weight as seen on personalized avatars veridically? I can answer this question by considering the amount of the BMI%

change of the avatar that the participants indicated as similar to their current weight. I determined the BMI% change values that corresponded to the maximum proportion of 'avatar is my weight' answers for each participant and visual cue (shape and texture) separately. The mean values are shown in Figure 39. I investigated the effect of the visual cues on the BMI% change values that corresponded to the maximum proportion of 'avatar is my weight' by performing an ANOVA with shape (own vs. average) and texture (own photo-realistic vs. checkerboard pattern) as within-subject factors and BMI% change (reported by the participant as their current weight) as the dependent measure. The underlying avatar's body shape had little influence (no significant effect) on the BMI% change, $F(1,12) = 0.342, p = 0.57$. Interestingly, the texture of the avatar significantly influenced BMI% change reported by the participant for their current weight estimates, $F(1,12) = 14.21, p = 0.003$. More specifically, participants reported that their weight was equivalent to the weight of an avatar with a significantly smaller BMI when the avatar was displayed with a checkerboard texture as compared to participants' own photo-realistic texture. The interaction between shape and texture was non-significant, $F(1,12) = 0.103, p = 0.753$.

There was a significant effect of the texture on the PSE

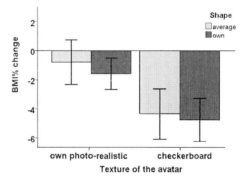

Figure 39: The point of subjective equality (PSE) in terms of BMI% change per experimental condition. Error bars represent ±1 standard error of the mean.

The above analyses suggest that people are able to veridically portray their current weight in the four types of avatars (own shape with own texture / own shape with checkerboard texture / average shape with own texture / average shape with checkerboard pattern texture) used for this experiment and that the point of subjective equalities (PSEs) are all slightly smaller than the participant's current weight (see Figure 39). But also, it is important to consider that there is a tolerance range for accepting an avatar as having the same weight as oneself. The tolerance range can be determined by considering the absolute difference between the PSEs (i.e., BMI% change that correspond to 0.5 answer proportion) on the psychometric functions fitted to the overweight and underweight data. Ranges for each texture and shape are shown in Figure 39.

The results indicated that there is a range of weights that participants accept as their current weight

The data suggests that for the avatars with own photo-realistic texture and average shape the range of the PSEs was between -2.21% and 0.83% BMI change, with own photo-realistic texture and own shape - between -0.52% and -2.64% BMI change, with checkerboard texture and average shape - between -2.63% and -5.95% BMI change and with checkerboard texture and own shape the range was between -3.17% and -6.05% BMI change.

7.2.3 *Method of adjustment for estimating current weight*

Additionally, I used the method of adjustment task for current weight (see Figure 40) as a converging measure for the one interval 2AFC procedure. If the method of adjustment provides consistent results with the 2AFC method this may be a better technique to use with the clinical population because it requires less time. Further, I used the method of adjustment task for ideal weight (see Figure 40) to determine whether there is a difference between the participants' perception of current and ideal weight. To analyze whether the visual cues (texture and shape) affected the method of adjustment task for both current and ideal weights, I ran a 2 (Texture: checkerboard vs. own photo-realistic) $\times$ 2 (Shape: own vs. average) $\times$ 2 (Task: current weight vs ideal weight) within-subjects, repeated measures ANOVA with mean estimated weight (BMI% change from the participant's current weight) as the dependent variable.

The results showed that the participants estimated their ideal weight to be significantly thinner than their estimated current weight, $F(1,47) = 28.390, p < 0.001, \eta_p^2 = 0.38$ (the means are shown in Figure 40). The shape and the texture, as well as the two- and three-way interactions between texture, shape, and task were not significant, all $ps > 0.16$. Even though I found no significant effect of the texture on participants' estimates of current and ideal body weight, there was a trend in the estimates that was consistent with the results from the 2AFC procedure. Namely, in order to make the avatar represent the requested weight (for both the ideal and current estimates) participants took more weight off the checkerboard-textured avatar than the avatar with the photo-realistic texture (compare Figure 40 to Figure 39). I also analyzed (using the same analyses as above, but a changed dependent variable) the amount of time participants took to complete the adjustment procedure for each task and condition. I found no differences in the time taken to complete the tasks, which suggests that time was not a factor in the observed differences in adjustment across tasks and texture, all $ps > 0.34$. I then investigated whether a relationship existed between the PSE (more specifically, the PSE for the positive direction - overweight avatar; and the PSE for the negative direction - underweight avatar) and the estimations from the method of adjustment task for current weight. I also found a positive correlation between the PSE for the positive direction (overweight avatar) and the estimates from the method of adjustment task for the current weight, $r(11) = 0.324, p = 0.032$. However, the relationship between the PSE for the negative direction (underweight avatar) and the method of adjustment estimates for the current weight was negative,

In the method of adjustment task participants estimated their ideal weight to be significantly smaller than current weight

There was a similar trend of the method of adjustment and the 2AFC estimations

$r(11) = -0.382, p = 0.011$. This suggests that the method of adjustment is a possible alternative time-saving method for measuring perceived body weight in personalized avatars.

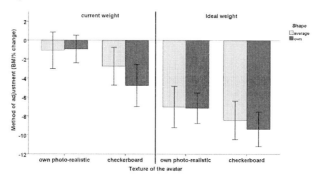

Figure 40: The average current weight (left) and ideal weight (right) as estimated by the method of adjustment per experimental condition in terms of BMI% change from the actual weight of the participant Error bars represent ± 1 standard error of the mean.

Further, for the mesh of each participant the distance between the participant's avatar and the average avatar in the body scan database using several measurements was calculated (see Table 7.1.1). First, the Mahalanobis distance between each participant's shape deformations and the average shape deformations, in terms of deformation coefficients β was calculated. Second, the uniqueness of the participant was estimated. Thus, we estimated the uniqueness of the participant compared to the average shape in terms of BMI (see height/weight distance in Table 7.1.1). Finally, the Mahalanobis distance of each participant in the distribution of 15 selected measurements spanned by the CAESAR bodies (bust-chest-circumference-under-bust, ankle-circumference, weight, waist-circumference-pref, shoulder-breadth, crotch-height, chest-circumference, thigh-circumference, spine-to-shoulder, hip-circumference-maximum, arm-length-shoulder-to-wrist, stature, knee-height, head-circumference, neck-base-circumference, including height and weight) (see selected measurements distance in Table 7.1.1)were calculated. Note, that the scale of the two calculated types of distance measures varies because Mahalanobis distances in spaces of different dimensionality were used.

I then investigated the relationship between the calculated distances, the slope and the PSEs. All of the correlations between distances and slopes or distances and PSEs were not significant, all $ps > 0.22$. The non-significant correlations suggest that regardless of the difference between the participant's own body and the average body, the participants were able to estimate their body weight veridically. This would suggest that for similar experiments (in which the participants are estimating own body weight) it is not necessary to

The analysis revealed no significant correlation between calculated distances, the slope and the PSEs

use the personalized 3D scan of the participant but rather is enough to use an average avatar which has the same height as the participant.

7.2.4 *Considering possible confounds*

I tested participants' self-esteem because it is a potential confounding variable in this experiment. For calculating the self-esteem of the participants I used the traditional Rosenberg's self-esteem scale which ranges from 0 to 30. According to Rosenberg's self-esteem scale scores between 15 and 25 are within the normal range, while scores smaller than 15 suggest low self-esteem and scores greater than 25 suggest high self-esteem. For the self-esteem questionnaire, the participants scored on average 21.75 ($SD = 5.578$, see Table 7.1.1 for participant's score range) with only two participants scoring below 15 and three participants scoring above 25. I examined participants whose self-esteem deviated from normal (smaller than 15 or greater than 25) and found that their psychophysical data was not significantly different from those in the normal range, all $ps > 0.356$. Thus, it is unlikely that differences in self-esteem drove the observed effects, but I do concede that the sample size is probably too small to make a strong claim here. Also, given the sample size was 13, the number of participants in this experiment does not provide enough power to detect meaningful correlations between self-esteem and the observed effects (see [215]). In the post-questionnaire participants were asked to report their ideal weight in kilograms and reported their ideal weight to be 57.69 kilograms on average (see Table 7.1.1). This is 2.99 kilograms less than their average weight. This corresponds to an average of -4.93% BMI change.

There was an effect of shape and texture on the questionnaire

Willingness to accept the avatar as similar to one's body could also have affected the results. The participants' ratings of the perceived similarity between their own body and the avatar that the participants estimated as similar to their current weight in each of the four sessions of the experiment are shown in Figure 41. I analyzed the data from the similarity questions using non-parametric tests, namely, Wilcoxon signed-rank tests with planned comparisons because the questionnaire data was not normally distributed. The tests indicated that the participants gave significantly lower ratings for similarity when the avatar had average shape compared to when it was the participant's exact shape, $z = -2.803, p = 0.005$ (means are shown in Figure 41). The ratings for the avatar with the checkerboard pattern texture were also significantly lower compared to the ratings for the avatar with the photo-realistic texture, $z = -2.805, p = 0.005$, (the means are shown in Figure 41).

In addition to the similarity questions I asked the participants whether they recognized the avatar. Their answer were as follows: avatar with own photo-realistic texture and own shape - answer "yes" ($N = 13$), answer "no" ($N = 0$); avatar with checkerboard texture and own shape - answer "yes" ($N = 10$), answer "no" ($N = 3$); avatar with own photo-realistic texture and average shape - answer "yes" ($N = 4$), answer "no" ($N = 9$); and avatar with checkerboard texture and average shape - answer "yes"($N = 1$), answer "no" ($N = 11$).

These results suggest that the participants were able to distinguish that the average avatar did not have their body shape.

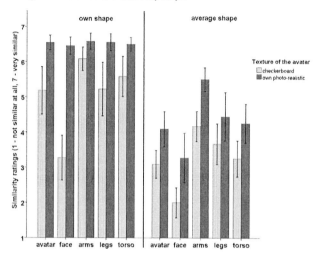

Figure 41: The similarity ratings for arms, avatar, face, legs and torso in the post-session questionnaires for each avatar. Error bars represent ±1 standard error of the mean.

7.3 DISCUSSION

To my knowledge, this is the first investigation of body weight perception conducted using both the participant's photo-realistic body textures and the participant's accurate 3D body shape. Moreover, I used state-of-the-art algorithms in order to present participants with convincing alternative body shapes that could represent their own shape if they lose or gain a certain amount of their body weight (BMI% change). The results suggest that women were more willing to accept thinner avatar bodies (smaller BMI than their current BMI) as most similar to their current weight, as compared to when the avatar had a bigger body than the participant's current body. Not surprisingly, these women were less tolerant of avatar body weights that were greater than their current BMI. This willingness to accept thinner avatar bodies as one's own was pronounced in the case of avatars presented with a checkerboard texture rather than a photo-realistic one, which parallels the results of Thompson and Mikellidou 2011 on the perception of the size of mannequins that was textured with vertical or horizontal lines. To my knowledge Thompson and Mikellidou 2011 research is the only prior study to this research that has examined the potential effects of visual cues, namely, the influence of the texture cues on perceived body size. My findings also show that the similar-

The results suggest that women are more willing to accept thinner avatar bodies as their current weight and even more so if the avatar is textured with a checkerboard texture

ity of the shape of the avatar (i.e., an avatar with the participant's own body shape vs. an avatar with average shape) did not have an effect on perceiving an avatar's body weight as similar to one's own. However, this finding was not completely surprising because even the average female avatar still had some anthropomorphic features of the participant, such as the same height, weight and BMI. Even though the results from the questionnaire show that the participants were able to distinguish that the average avatar did not have their body shape, they still veridically estimated their body weight when the avatar had average shape. Thus, the results suggest that the participants would accept an average avatar that had an equivalent BMI (i.e., height and weight) as a representation of their own weight.

Participants accept an average avatar that had an equivalent BMI (i.e., height and weight) as a representation of their own weight

The findings showed that the participants perceived veridically their body weight when the avatar had own photo-realistic texture and either average or own body shape. These results are consistent with the findings from previous research that investigated the perception of own body size [82], using distorted photographs of the participants' bodies. One reason people may have perceived in the experiment their body more veridically with the photo-realistic texture is that this texture does carry some lighting information (though only a small amount due to uniform lighting from all directions when captured). Thus, the photo-realistic texture provides shape from shading information which might provide additional shape cues. The clothes on the body also provide shape information. Thus, the photo-realistic texture allows one to see more local shape features to guide estimates. In contrast to the photo-realistic texture which portrays shape-specific features, such as small wrinkles and irregularities of the shape, the checkerboard texture has no directional lighting information and masks some of these features. This suggests that the quality of the texture and the amount of information that it provides, has an influence on the belief or desires about the person's own body weight. Another potential reason for the influence of texture on weight perception of these avatars is the fact that the photo-realistic texture provides also more detailed information about face specific features (e.g. eyes color, mouth color). The texture on the face may have simply drawn the attention of the participant to the changes in the both face shape and body shape, regardless of how similar the avatar was perceived to be to the participant, resulting in a greater accuracy of estimated weight.

The quality of the texture and the amount of information that it provides, has an influence on perception of body weight

This study represents an initial step toward understanding perception of own body as depicted by personalized avatars. While promising, the observed results leave open many questions for future work. For example, if the avatar portrayed considerable changes in body dimensions as compared to the women's true body size or shape, it is possible that there would be an effect of the shape on the perception of body weight. Future work is planned to assess whether other changes to body dimension (e.g. height, shoulder width, limb length, etc.) could have more of an effect on the similarity of an avatar's body weight to one's own.

Experiments which use personalized avatars could provide new insights about the impact of perspective (e.g. $1^{st}PP$ and $3^{rd}PP$ using HMD and LSIDs) or orientation on the perception of body weight. Additionally, investigating perception of body weight using men will provide more information as to whether the results of this experiment can generalize to men as well, or similar to other research there will be difference in perception of weight between men and women, as well as people who have recently gained or lost a substantial amount of weight.

7.4   SUMMARY OF THE MAIN FINDINGS

- Women perceive their body weight veridical as portrayed on a personalized self-avatar on a LSID.

- Women are more willing to accept a thinner body (smaller BMI) as most similar to their actual body weight, as compared to bigger body.

- The range of weights that women perceive as similar to their current weight is within -6% to 0.8% of the users current BMI

- The texture of the self-avatar can be used to influence perception of own body weight.

8

8.1 EXPERIENCE OF OWNERSHIP OVER A CONSIDERABLY DIFFERENT SELF-AVATAR IN VR

The research in Chapter 5 extends the knowledge about embodiment in VR and shows that women can experience a sense of *ownership, agency* and *self − localization* over a stylized static self-avatar of a considerably different size than the participant. In contrast to other researchers who have used 1st PP virtual avatars and employed the RHI paradigm in VR, in this study I used questions related to agency. My findings suggest that the participant's sense of agency and ownership is influenced by the combination of proprioceptive and somatosensory feedback from the *physical* body and the cues provided from the head-tracking and the 1st PP self-avatar in a similar posture. It is possible that participants are trying to integrate the perceived (from VR and reality) stimuli into one coherent percept.

The self-avatar should not have the same size as the participant in order for the participant to identify with the self-avatar

Additionally, both body (body size estimations) and space (affordance estimations) perception in VR were influenced by the stimuli. Though there was no effect of visual-tactile stimulation on the affordance and body size estimations, the analysis showed that even before the visual-tactile stimulation the participants perceived a change in their *experienced* body dimensions (consistent with the size of the virtual body). The affordance and body size estimates for the *experienced* body were influenced by the visual stimulus (the size of the 1st PP *virtual* body). The affordance and body size estimates for the *physical* body show that, if instructed, participants can dissociate visual feedback from perceived proprioceptive feedback and memory of their *physical* body.

Both body and space perception in VR are influenced by the VR setup

8.2 DESIGNING LSID VR SYSTEMS TO PROVIDE A REALISTIC EXPERIENCE

Similar to HMD VEs, I found that egocentric distances in the LSIDs are overall significantly underestimated, as compared to the overall veridical estimations in the real world. In the flat LSID, I specifically investigated the role of stereoscopic projection and motion parallax on egocentric distance estimations. The findings indicated that stereoscopic depth cues do create less underestimation but only for the nearest distance. I found that even when providing motion parallax and stereoscopic depth cues to the observer, egocentric distance estimates were overall still underestimated. The results indicated a pattern of effect of distance to the target on the distance judgments. Further research is necessary to explore the reason why this effect is not always the

There is distance underestimation in LSIDs

The pattern of distance effect is not the same throughout all LSIDs

same throughout different displays and not all LSIDs show the same distance effect as compared to the real world.

8.3   THE CONTRIBUTION OF VISUAL CUES AND THE PRECISION OF PERCEPTION OF OWN BODY WEIGHT PORTRAYED BY A PERSONALIZED SELF-AVATAR

Veridical perception of body weight - range within 0.8 to −6 BMI% change

This research demonstrates that using state-of-the-art personalized avatars for assessing body perception is beneficial for gaining a better understanding of the influence of visual cues on body perception. The results presented in Chapter 7 showed that the participants were more sensitive to changes of body weight when the avatar had higher weight than the participant, as compared to when the avatar was thinner than the participant. This suggests that participants are willing to accept a thinner body (smaller BMI) as most similar to their actual body weight. The BMI range (within 0.8 to −6 BMI% change from the participant's BMI) that our participants accepted as their current weight is smaller than in other literature, such as Hashimoto & Iriki 2013. This might be due to the more realistic visual stimuli that I used or the fact that the intervals between the different BMIs that I used were smaller than the intervals used in Hashimoto & Iriki 2013. Another reason could be that due to the approach that I used for implementing the method of adjustment task the participants were more precise. This might also be a reason why the results from the method of adjustment task had a similar trend as the analysis of the PSE (2AFC task). However, further research is necessary for more conclusive results (see Section 9.4).

Body perception is influenced by the texture of the avatar

In addition, both the shape and the texture had an effect on the reported similarity of the body parts and the whole avatar to the participant's body. Nevertheless, I found that the shape of the avatar had little effect on the perception of body weight and body weight was perceived veridically regardless of shape. A reason for this could be that I used an average female shape rather than a shape which was significantly different from those of the participants. Interestingly, I found that the perception of body weight can be influenced by the texture of the avatar. Specifically, the avatars with checkerboard texture needed to be significantly thinner than the avatars with photo-realistic texture in order to represent the participant's current weight. The participants perceived their body weight veridically when they saw their own photo-realistic texture. Another interesting finding of this experiment is that the participants have not recognized their own texture when used on the average avatar. However, further investigation on this is necessary to make conclusive statements as to whether any photo-realistic texture can be used for veridical perception of weight. Additionally, more insights about the effect of other textures on perception of body weight will be very useful for researchers and physicians who are interested in using realistic self-avatar to investigate body perception.

9

IMPLICATIONS FOR COMPUTER GRAPHICS AND VIRTUAL REALITY APPLICATIONS

The findings of this research can be used to improve the design, programming and visualization of the content of VR applications, such as games, clinical VR or virtual try-on applications for the clothing industry. In this chapter, I list the implications of this research that are related for improving the user's perceptual experience and the self-avatars in VR applications. Also, I discuss several implications and general suggestions related to researchers interested in investigating and manipulating body and space perception in VR.

9.1 IMPLICATIONS FOR DESIGNING LSID VR SYSTEMS TO PROVIDE A REALISTIC EXPERIENCE

The findings presented in Chapter 6 can be used to improve the VR experience of the user in terms of depth perception. More specifically, it would be useful for the researchers and the developers of VR applications to determine the amount of distance underestimation using a real world scene as a control condition and a replication of the real world scene for the VE. In addition to this standard procedure for estimating depth perception, it is beneficial to use a large range of distances to determine a pattern of distance effect for a given LSID, especially if the aim is to achieve veridical perception of the LSID VE.

Based on my findings I provide suggestions for creating perceptual experience of depth similar to that of the real world

First, in case only one object of interest in the VE (such as a self-avatar) should be perceived veridically, then the optimal position of this object would be at the distance which was perceived closest to veridical. Second, to create a veridical perceptual experience of depth in the entire virtual scene the overall judgments should be evaluated. If the pattern of distance is the same, then depending on the overall results one can perform an adaptation task. The research of Mohler et al. [185] and Richardson & Waller [186] in HMD VEs proposed using corrective feedback for overcoming spatial underestimation or using an adaptation task. Another alternative would be distortion of the geometric FOV [189] or a change in the virtual eye height [190] in order to compensate for the mismatch (under- or overestimation of distances) between the perception of the real world and the VE.

If the pattern of distance effect in the VE is different than the one in the real world (see Section 6.4 for possible explanations), further investigation is necessary to determine the cause of this mismatch and whether the specifications of the LSID or the VR setup should be modified in order to achieve veridical perception.

If the pattern of distance effect is not the same as the one in the real world, further investigation of the cause is necessary

9.2   IMPLICATIONS FOR VR APPLICATIONS IN WHICH IT IS IMPORTANT FOR THE USER TO IDENTIFY WITH THEIR SELF-AVATAR

The findings of Chapter 5 show that it is not always necessary for the user's stylized self-avatar in the HMD VE to have the same size (in terms of weight) as the user in order to have an influence on the user's perception. Specifically, it is sufficient for the VR system to fulfill the following criteria:

There are certain criteria that VR system should fulfill to influence the user's body perception and perception of their action capabilities in VR

1. The VR system should provide a visual feedback of the self-avatar similar to the location where the user expects their physical body to be, i.e. the avatar should be rendered from a 1st PP.

2. The 1st PP self-avatar should have similar posture as the user.

3. The VR system should provide head-tracking of the user.

Thus, the provided sensory (e.g. visual stimuli, head tracking, somatosensory information) feedback is enough to influence both the perception of body size and actions in the VR. This can be especially beneficial for VR applications (such as clinical VR, training or entertainment), in which it is important for the user to identify with the avatar's body. The above mentioned properties could be intuitively implemented in any VR applications, which use customizable self-avatars and HMD, such as the Oculus Rift [84], for projecting the visual content. Additionally, further research is necessary to make conclusive statements as to whether it is beneficial that the height, the legs, the torso and the arm length of the stylized self-avatar should the same as the user's.

My research provides important methodological distinction between three body types (physical, experienced and virtual) useful for body perception research that uses the RHI paradigm

The distinction between the three body types (*physical*, *experienced* and *virtual*) that I introduce in Chapter 5 is an important methodological aspect for VR experiments that employ the RHI paradigm. It can be also used by body perception researchers to collect judgments based on specific cues that influence body perception. Thus one can have a better understanding of which cues (e.g. visual, proprioceptive, somatosensory, memory or a combination thereof) have a greater impact on body perception and whether it varies between different setups.

9.3   IMPLICATIONS FOR VR APPLICATIONS THAT USE PERSONALIZED SELF-AVATARS

9.3.1   *The contribution of visual cues and the properties of the body morphology to the perception of a personalized self-avatar*

Developers could consider the listed features when aiming at veridical perception of personalized avatars

The results of my research suggest that there are perceptual tasks, like perception of one's own body weight, for which it is not necessary to use the individual's own personalized self-avatar in order for them to veridically perceive their weight. These results have direct implications for VR applications (such as ergonomics [198], clinical VR [85] or clothing industry [199]) which use personalized avatars and aim at veridical body perception. The results from

Chapter 7 demonstrated that visual cues, such as texture cues, influence the user's perception of the weight of their personalized self-avatar in VR. Based on my findings I list several features that contribute to veridical perception of body weight in VR:

- Texture cues - the quality of the texture and the amount of information that it provides, has an influence on the perceived body weight. Changing the texture of the self-avatar can be used to achieve perceptual similarity in terms of weight. Specifically, photo-realistic texture is necessary for veridical perception of body weight of the personalized self-avatar. A checkerboard texture can be used if the avatar needs to be perceived about 2.9% bigger that it actually is.

- Shape cues - besides the personalized self-avatar with the user's shape, a personalized self-avatar with average shape and the user's height can be used for veridical perception of body weight.

- Weight - the self-avatar should have the user's height and the weight of the self-avatar should be within -6% to 0.8% of the users current BMI regardless of shape (either one's own body morphology or average body morphology)

Therefore, many VR applications which use personalized avatars will be beneficial from a database of average avatars. Such database will provide low-cost customizable and realistic personalized self-avatars for various VR applications. Using such database and considering the results of my research, the personalized avatars of the users could be used overtime, if their personalized avatar:

It is not necessary to scan the users of VR applications each time before using it

- has the user's height and the weight of the self-avatar is within -6% to 0.8% of the user's current BMI regardless of shape (either own body morphology or average body morphology)

- has the user's height and is textured, so that the weight of the self-avatar is perceived to have from -6% to 0.8% deviation of the user's current BMI.

Thus, it is only necessary to weigh the users before using the VR application. If the self-avatar is within the above mentioned range the user can directly use the VR tool. Otherwise, the user could be scanned or the user's self-avatar can be modified according to the suggestions listed above.

9.3.2 *Implications for clinical VR tools*

Similar setup to the one used in Chapter 7 can be used to evaluate body perception of patients

The methods used in Chapter 7 can be directly applied for clinical VR tools used in therapies to help the physician to evaluate body perception of patients diagnosed with stroke, anorexia nervosa or obesity. In such VR tools it is important that the representation of the participant's body is as accurate as possible. Therefore, personalized avatars can be used to investigate patients' perception of body size and shape. Thus, the physician can precisely assess the difference between the individual's perceived and current body size or limb size.

Additionally, the findings of my research can be useful for programmers that develop clinical VR tools which are used by physicians in therapies which aim to minimize the discrepancy between the perceived and the actual body (or limb) size of patients with body image disorders. The developers of such VR tools could implement self-avatars with customizable texture cues, such that when visually manipulated the texture cues gradually change to fit the patient's perceived body size. Thus, VR applications can be integrated in therapies to provide the patients an alternative experience of their body. Such applications can be used to help patients to accept their actual body size and minimize the discrepancy between their perceived and actual body size. Still, the impact of visual cues, such as texture or shape, may vary between different setups. Therefore, it is important to investigate whether there is a difference in perception of weight in VEs presented on HMD (where the participants no longer have visual information about their own physical body), as compared to LSIDs.

The results of this thesis could be used to develop clinical VR applications that aim at minimizing the discrepancy between perceived and actual body by providing the patients an alternative experience of their body

9.3.3   Clothing-fashion industry

The finding from Chapter 7 can be useful for both clothing companies and designers. Specifically, similar setup as the one that I used in Chapter 7 could be used to gain better understanding of the impact of clothes on the perception of body weight, which could have commercial value. Instead of scanning each customer and providing them with their own personalized avatars, average personalized avatars can be used for try on and visualization of cloths by shops and on-line stores to speed up the shopping process. Furthermore, if the shops have an access to a database of personalized avatars it might be even possible to use avatars which body morphology is similar to the user's without the need of scanning the customer. Additionally, the companies that use 3D body scans do not have to scan their customers every time. The customer's personalized avatar could be used overtime if the customer's weight is within the specific range found in Chapter 7.

Personalized avatars with average shape can be used by clothing companies to speed up the shopping process

9.4   IMPLICATIONS FOR NOVEL RESPONSE MEASURES IN CLINICAL VR AND BODY PERCEPTION RESEARCH

I have used affordance judgments in an attempt to find a more reliable measure for ownership and embodiment. Since affordances are indirect measure of body size, affordance judgments might be a promising matter for further investigation with respect to finding new measures for embodiment. The procedure I used did not have an effect on the affordance estimations. However, it is possible that in order to find an effect of the manipulation on the affordance estimations, a different protocol or type of an affordance measure has to be used.

New response measures for investigating body perception and embodiment

In Chapter 7 I used both the method of adjustment task as well as a psychophysics procedure to assess body perception. Further, investigation is necessary in order to provide conclusive results as to whether the method of adjustment task for body estimations can be as reliable as the psychophysics procedure. The implications of a research that investigates the reliability of the method of adjustment task with respect to body perception will be important for clinical VR to shorten (in terms of time) experimental procedures.

In Chapters 5 and 7 I use morphs of the 3D mesh of personalized or stylized self-avatars to enable the participants to smoothly and precisely adjust the 3D shape of the avatar in the method of adjustment task. Even though morphs of the 3D mesh have been used in various fields (e.g. animation, computer graphics), to my knowledge similar approach in the body perception research has only been used in the research of Normand et al. [78] to adjust only the belly of the self-avatar. Therefore, the implementation and the findings of my research are useful for researchers interested in understanding the influence of the self-avatar on the perception in VR. Furthermore, my research might be of interest to researchers developing new response measures and new strategies for VR therapies to more precisely evaluate body perception of patients with body image disorders (see Section 9.3.2). Additionally, considering the sensitivity of some patients about their body size, the developers of clinical VR can implement and explore the usefulness of new response measures, such as affordance measure (as the one used in Chapter 5), to gain new insights in the perception of patients with eating disorders.

Morphing of 3D body models can be integrated in response measures assessing body perception for clinical VR applications

The novel approach for assessing body perception using realistic personalized avatars that I propose and use in Chapter 7, can also be used to develop and investigate new approaches for measuring perceptual similarity while varying visual cues. Additionally, it would be interesting to use an avatar with a significantly different shape rather than the average shape in order to directly manipulate task difficulty and investigate whether such manipulations could also lead to a bias towards a lower BMI when estimating one's own weight. Finally, it is also possible that the impact of visual cues like shape and texture can vary between different setups, especially because HMD VEs the participants no longer have visual information about their physical body, instead, they receive visual information about the body of the avatar.

Measuring perceptual similarity using a realistic 3D body model

10

CONCLUSION

In this thesis I investigated body and self-avatar perception and their influence on perceived space using VR. I considered the advantages and the limitations of current VR applications (Chapter 1) and body and space perception literature (Chapter 2), as well as the benefits of state-of-the-art technology (Chapter 2) for the design and the implementation of the experiments presented in Chapters 5, 6 and 7. Then, I used the main findings of my research to discuss ways to influence the user's body and space perception in VR (Chapter 8) and their implications (Chapter 9) that relate to computer graphics, clinical VR, clothing industry and body and space perception research in VR.

My research showed that users can adapt to the dimensions of their self-avatar, even if the stylized self-avatar has a considerably different weight (see Chapter 5). Thus, it is not always necessary for the developers of computer games, VR tools (clinical, entertainment or industry) to create avatars that are as similar as possible to the user's body to enable the users to identify with their self-avatars. It is sufficient to provide sensory feedback, such as: 1) a 1st PP stylized self-avatar in a similar posture to the participant; and 2) visualize the VE using head-tracking in an HMD. This approach can be applied to improve the usefulness of clinical VR applications for VR therapies and diagnostics.

The users can adapt to the dimensions of their self-avatar and their perception of actions in VR can be biased by the size of the stylized self-avatar

The experiments that I conducted to determine the optimal position (with respect to veridical perception in VR, see Chapter 6) of the personalized self-avatars in Chapter 7 indicated that distances in LSIDs are underestimated, as compared to the nearly veridical distance perception in the real world. I also found an effect of distance to the target on the accuracy of distance estimations, which was not always the same for the tested LSIDs and the real world. These findings provide new insights that are useful for developers of VR applications and researchers interested in designing LSID VR systems to provide a realistic experience in the VR.

Distance judgments in LSIDs are underestimated and their accuracy depends on the position of the target

Finally, in Chapter 7 I found that weight was perceived veridically regardless of body shape, even though the participants estimated the avatar with average shape to be less similar to their body shape as compared to the avatar with their own shape. Interestingly, the texture of the self-avatar influenced perception of body weight, so that avatars with a checkerboard texture appeared significantly bigger than those with a photo-realistic texture. There is a range within (-6% to 0.8% of the users current BMI) which the weight of the personalized self-avatar is perceived to be the same as the user's weight.

The texture influences perception of body weight and there is a range within which the weight is perceived veridically regardless of body shape

This research provides new insights for developing new response measures and understanding body perception of patients with body image disorders. More specifically, morphing of 3D body models can be integrated in response measures assessing body perception for clinical VR applications. The findings of my research could be used for developing of clinical VR applications

My research can be of interest to researchers and developers of VR applications (e.g. games, clinical VR or clothing industry)

that aim at minimizing the discrepancy between perceived and actual body, and provide the patients an alternative experience of their body. Furthermore, my findings can be of interest to developers of personalized avatars for games, clinical VR, virtual try-on applications for the clothing industry or other VR applications for entertainment or scientific purposes.

[1] K. Harris. Collected quotes from Albert Einstein, 2014. URL http:
//rescomp.stanford.edu/~cheshire/EinsteinQuotes.html.
Copyright: Kevin Harris 1995.

[2] A. 'Skip' Rizzo, J. Difede, B. O. Rothbaum, G. Reger, J. Spitalnick,
J. Cukor, and R. Mclay. Development and early evaluation of the
virtual iraq/afghanistan exposure therapy system for combat-related
ptsd. *Annals of the New York Academy of Sciences*, 1208(1):114–125,
2010. ISSN 1749-6632. doi: 10.1111/j.1749-6632.2010.05755.x. URL
http://dx.doi.org/10.1111/j.1749-6632.2010.05755.x.

[3] T. Ni, G. S. Schmidt, O. G. Staadt, M. A. Livingston, R. Ball, and
R. May. A survey of large high-resolution display technologies, techniques, and applications. In *Proceedings of the IEEE conference on Virtual Reality*, VR 2006, pages 223–236, Washington, DC, USA, 2006.
IEEE Computer Society.

[4] A. A. Rizzo, D. Klimchuk, R. Mitura, T. Bowerly, J. G. Buckwalter,
R. Katherine, R. Adams, P. Finn, I. Tarnanas, T. H. Ollendick, and S.-
C. Yeh. A virtual reality scenario for all seasons: the virtual classroom.
CNS Spectrum, 11:35–44, 2006.

[5] M. Slater. Place illusion and plausibility can lead to realistic behaviour
in immersive virtual environments. *Philos Trans R Soc Lond B Biol
Sci*, 364(1535):3549–57, 2009.

[6] I.V. Alexandrova, M. Rall, M. Breidt, U. Kloos, G. Tullius, H.H.
Bülthoff, and B.J. Mohler. Animations of medical training scenarios in
immersive virtual environments. In *Digital Media and Digital Content
Management (DMDCM), 2011 Workshop on*, pages 9–12, May 2011.
doi: 10.1109/DMDCM.2011.64.

[7] I.V. Alexandrova, M. Rall, M. Breidt, G. Tullius, U. Kloos, H.H.
Bülthoff, and B.J. Mohler. Enhancing medical communication training using motion capture, perspective taking and virtual reality. In
*Medicine Meets Virtual Reality 19: NextMed, 19th Medicine Meets Vir-
tual Reality Conference (MMVR 2012)*, pages 16–22, February 2012.

[8] G. J. Carrougher, H. G. Hoffman, D. Nakamura, D. Lezotte, M. Soltani,
L. Leahy, L. H. Engrav, and D. R. Patterson. The effect of virtual reality
on pain and range of motion in adults with burn injuries. *J Burn Care
Res*, 30(5):785–791, Sep-Oct 2009.

[9] W. Swartout, J. Gratch, R. W. Hill, E. Hovy, S. Marsella, J. Rickel, and
D. Traum. Toward virtual humans. *AI Mag.*, 27:96–108, July 2006.

[10] S. Jayaram, H. I. Connacher, and K. W. Lyons. Virtual assembly using virtual reality techniques. *Computer-Aided Design*, 29(8):575–584, 1997. URL http://www.sciencedirect.com/science/article/pii/S0010448596000942.

[11] E. van Wyk and R. de Villiers. Virtual reality training applications for the mining industry. In *Proceedings of the 6th International Conference on Computer Graphics, Virtual Reality, Visualization and Interaction in Africa*, AFRIGRAPH 2009, pages 53–63, New York, NY, USA, 2009. ACM.

[12] G. Riva. From virtual to real body: Virtual reality as embodied technology. *Journal of CyberTherapy and Rehabilitiation*, 1:7–22, 2008.

[13] G. Riva. Virtual reality in psychotherapy: Review. *CyberPsychology and Behavior*, 8:220–230, 2005.

[14] M. Slater, B. Lotto, M. Arnold, and M. V. Sanchez-Vives. How we experience immersive virtual environments: the concept of presence and its measurement. *Anuario de Psicologia*, 40(2):193–210, 2009.

[15] M. Slater, P. Khanna, J. Mortensen, and I. Yu. Visual realism enhances realistic response in an immersive virtual environment. *IEEE Comput. Graph. Appl.*, 29(3):76–84, May 2009.

[16] Insu Yu, J. Mortensen, P. Khanna, B. Spanlang, and M. Slater. Visual realism enhances realistic response in an immersive virtual environment - part 2. *Computer Graphics and Applications, IEEE*, 32(6): 36–45, Nov 2012. ISSN 0272-1716. doi: 10.1109/MCG.2012.121.

[17] E. McManus, B. Bodenheimer, S. de la Rosa, S. Streuber, H. H. Bülthoff, and B. J. Mohler. The influence of avatar animation (self and other) on distance estimation, object interaction and locomotion in an immersive virtual environment. In *Proceedings of the ACM SIGGRAPH Symposium on Applied Perception in Graphics and Visualization*, APGV 2011, pages 37–44, New York, NY, USA, 2011. ACM.

[18] J. M. Loomis, J. A. Da Silva, N. Fujita, and S. S. Fukusima. Visual space perception and visually directed action. *Journal of Experimental Psychology: Human Perception and Performance*, 18(4):906–921, 1992.

[19] J. W. Philbeck and J. M. Loomis. Comparison of two indicators of perceived egocentric distance under full-cue and reduced-cue conditions. *Journal of Experimental Psychology: Human Perception and Performance*, 23(1):72–85, 1997.

[20] J. M. Plumert, J. K. Kearney, J. F. Cremer, and K. Recker. Distance perception in real and virtual environments. *ACM Transactions on Applied Perception*, 2(3):216–233, 2005.

[21] E. Klein, J. E. Swan, G. S. Schmidt, M. A. Livingston, and O. G. Staadt. Measurement protocols for medium-field distance perception in large-screen immersive displays. In *IEEE Virtual Reality Conference*, VR 2009, pages 107–113, Washington, DC, USA, 2009. IEEE Computer Society.

[22] T. Y. Grechkin, T. D. Nguyen, J. M. Plumert, J. F. Cremer, and J. K. Kearney. How does presentation method and measurement protocol affect distance estimation in real and virtual environments? *ACM Transactions on Applied Perception*, 7:26:1–26:18, July 2010.

[23] J. E. Cutting and P. M. Vishton. *Perceiving layout and knowing distances: the integration, relative potency and contextual use of different information about depth*, volume 5: Perception of Space and Motion. 1995.

[24] B. J. Mohler, S. H. Creem-Regehr, and W. B. Thompson. The Influence of Feedback on Egocenteric Distance Judgments in Real and Virtual Environments. In *Proceedings of the ACM SIGGRAPH Symposium on Applied Perception in Graphics and Visualization*, APGV 2006, pages 9–14, New York, NY, USA, 2006. ACM.

[25] S. H. Creem-Regehr, P. Willemsen, A. A. Gooch, and W. B. Thompson. The Influence of Restricted Viewing Conditions on Egocentric Distance Perception: Implications for Real and Virtual Environments. *Perception*, 34(2):191–204, 2005.

[26] C. S. Sahm, S. H. Creem-Regehr, W. B. Thompson, and P. Willemsen. Throwing versus walking as indicators of distance perception in similar real and virtual environments. *ACM Transactions on Applied Perception*, 2(1):35–45, 2005.

[27] J. M. Loomis and J. Knapp. *Virtual and Adaptive Environments: Visual Perception of Egocentric Distance in Real and Virtual Environments*. Erlbaum, Mahwah, NJ, 2003.

[28] P. Willemsen, M. B. Colton, S. H. Creem-Regehr, and W. B. Thompson. The effects of head-mounted display mechanical properties and field-of-view on distance judgments in virtual environments. *ACM Transactions on Applied Perception*, 6(2):8:1–8:14, 2009.

[29] J. M. Knapp and J. M. Loomis. Limited field of view of head-mounted displays is not the cause of distance underestimation in virtual environments. *Presence: Teleoperators & Virtual Environments*, 13(5):572–577, 2004.

[30] V. Interrante, B. Ries, J. Lindquist, M. Kaeding, and L. Anderson. Elucidating factors that can facilitate veridical spatial perception in immersive virtual environments. *Presence: Teleoperators & Virtual Environments*, 17(2):176–198, 2008.

[31] J. A. Da Silva. Scales for perceived egocentric distance in a large open field: comparison of three psychophysical methods. *The American journal of psychology*, 98(1):119–144, 1985.

[32] R. McDonnell and C. O'Sullivan. Movements and voices affect perceived sex of virtual conversers. In *Proceedings of the 7th Symposium on Applied Perception in Graphics and Visualization*, APGV '10, pages 125–128, New York, NY, USA, 2010. ACM. ISBN 978-1-4503-0248-7. doi: 10.1145/1836248.1836272.

[33] C. Ennis, R. McDonnell, and C. O'Sullivan. Seeing is believing: Body motion dominates in multisensory conversations. In *ACM SIGGRAPH 2010 Papers*, SIGGRAPH '10, pages 91:1–91:9, New York, NY, USA, 2010. ACM. ISBN 978-1-4503-0210-4. doi: 10.1145/1833349.1778828.

[34] Z. Kasap and N. Magnenat-Thalmann. Intelligent virtual humans with autonomy and personality: State-of-the-art. In Nadia Magnenat-Thalmann, LakhmiC. Jain, and Nikhil Ichalkaranje, editors, *New Advances in Virtual Humans*, volume 140 of *Studies in Computational Intelligence*, pages 43–84. Springer Berlin Heidelberg, 2008. ISBN 978-3-540-79867-5. doi: 10.1007/978-3-540-79868-2_2.

[35] D. Traum, W. Swartout, J. Gratch, and S. Marsella. A virtual human dialogue model for non-team interaction. In L. Dybkjar and W. Minker, editors, *Recent Trends in Discourse and Dialogue*, volume 39 of *Text, Speech and Language Technology*, pages 45–67. Springer Netherlands, 2008. ISBN 978-1-4020-6820-1. doi: 10.1007/978-1-4020-6821-8_3.

[36] I. V. Alexandrova. Generating virtual humans using predefined bodily and facial emotions in real-time virtual environments, 2011.

[37] I. V. Piryankova, H. Y. Wong, S. A. Linkenauger, C. Stinson, M. R. Longo, H. H. Bülthoff, and B. J. Mohler. Owning an overweight or underweight body: Distinguishing the physical, experienced and virtual body. *PLoS ONE*, 9:e103428, 08 2014.

[38] I. V. Piryankova, J. K. Stefanucci, J. Romero, S. De La Rosa, M. J. Black, and B. J. Mohler. Can I recognize my body's weight? the influence of shape and texture on the perception of self. *ACM Trans. Appl. Percept.*, 11(3):13:1–13:18, September 2014. ISSN 1544-3558. doi: 10.1145/2641568.

[39] B. J. Mohler, S. H. Creem-Regehr, W. B. Thompson, and H. H. Bülthoff. The effect of viewing a self-avatar on distance judgments in an hmd-based virtual environment. *Presence: Teleoperators & Virtual Environments*, pages 230–242, 2010.

[40] T. J. Dodds, B. J. Mohler, and H. H. Bülthoff. Talk to the virtual hands: Self-animated avatars improve communication in head-mounted dis-

play virtual environments. *PLoS ONE*, 6(10):e25759, 10 2011. doi: 10.1371/journal.pone.0025759.

[41] S. Grogan. *Body image: understanding body dissatisfaction in men, women, and children - 2nd ed.* Routledge, 2007.

[42] J. Croll, D. Neumark-Sztainer, M. Story, and M. Ireland. Prevalence and risk and protective factors related to disordered eating behaviors among adolescents: relationship to gender and ethnicity. *Journal of Adolescent Health*, 31(2):166 – 175, 2002.

[43] L. N. Forrest. The role of perception in eating disorders, 2012.

[44] A. Artaud. *The Theater and Its Double*. Grove Press, 1958. ISBN 0-8021-5030-6.

[45] W. B. Thompson, R. Fleming, S. Creem-Regehr, and J. K. Stefanucci. *Visual perception from a computer graphics perspective*. A K Peters/CRC Press, 2011.

[46] L.M. Heilig. Stereoscopic-television apparatus for individual use, October 4 1960. URL https://www.google.com/patents/US2955156. US Patent 2,955,156.

[47] L. M. Heilig. Sensorama simulator, August 28 1962. URL http://www.google.com/patents/US3050870. US Patent 3,050,870.

[48] A. Li, Z. Montaniso, V. J. Chen, and J. I. Gold. Virtual reality and pain management: current trends and future directions. *Pain Management*, 1(2):147–157, Mar. 2011.

[49] I. E. Sutherland. The ultimate display. In *Proceedings of the IFIP Congress*, pages 506–508, 1965.

[50] W. E. Disney. Rocket ship amusement apparatus, November 25 1958. URL http://www.google.com/patents/US2861806. US Patent 2,861,806.

[51] N. Ducheneaut, M.-H. Wen, N. Yee, and G. Wadley. Body and mind: A study of avatar personalization in three virtual worlds. In *Proceedings of the SIGCHI Conference on Human Factors in Computing Systems*, CHI '09, pages 1151–1160, New York, NY, USA, 2009. ACM. ISBN 978-1-60558-246-7. doi: 10.1145/1518701.1518877.

[52] Blizzard Entertainment. World of warcraft, 2014. URL http://us.battle.net/wow/en/.

[53] Jr. Brooks, F.P. What's real about virtual reality? *Computer Graphics and Applications, IEEE*, 19(6):16–27, Nov 1999. ISSN 0272-1716. doi: 10.1109/38.799723.

[54] M. Mine. Towards virtual reality for the masses: 10 years of research at disney's vr studio. In *Proceedings of the Workshop on Virtual Environments 2003*, EGVE '03, pages 11–17, New York, NY, USA, 2003. ACM. ISBN 1-58113-686-2. doi: 10.1145/769953.769955. URL http://doi.acm.org/10.1145/769953.769955.

[55] M. Paranandi and T. Sarawgi. Virtual reality on architecture: Enabling possibilities. In *Proceedings of the 7th International Conference on Computer Aided Architectural Design Research in Asia*, CAADRIA 2002, pages 309–316, 18-20 April 2002. ISBN ISBN 983-2473-42-X.

[56] N. Negroponte. *Being Digital*. Alfred A Knopf, New York, 1995.

[57] W. A. Abdelhameed. Virtual reality use in architectural design studios: A case of studying structure and construction. *Procedia Computer Science*, 25(0):220 – 230, 2013. ISSN 1877-0509. doi: http://dx.doi.org/10.1016/j.procs.2013.11.027. 2013 International Conference on Virtual and Augmented Reality in Education.

[58] A Kotranza, Benjamin Lok, C.M. Pugh, and D.S. Lind. Virtual humans that touch back: Enhancing nonverbal communication with virtual humans through bidirectional touch. In *Virtual Reality Conference, 2009. VR 2009. IEEE*, pages 175–178, March 2009. doi: 10.1109/VR.2009.4811019.

[59] B. Lok, R. E. Ferdig, A. Raij, K. Johnsen, R. Dickerson, J. Coutts, A. Stevens, and D. S. Lind. Applying virtual reality in medical communication education: Current findings and potential teaching and learning benefits of immersive virtual patients. *Virtual Real.*, 10(3):185–195, November 2006. ISSN 1359-4338. doi: 10.1007/s10055-006-0037-3.

[60] H. Sabri, B. Cowan, B. Kapralos, M. Porte, D. Backstein, and A. Dubrowskie. Serious games for knee replacement surgery procedure education and training. *Procedia - Social and Behavioral Sciences*, 2(2):3483 – 3488, 2010. ISSN 1877-0428. doi: http://dx.doi.org/10.1016/j.sbspro.2010.03.539. Innovation and Creativity in Education.

[61] TüPASS. Tüpass, 2014. URL http://www.tupass.de.

[62] B. Cowan, M. Shelley, H. Sabri, B. Kapralos, A. Hogue, M. Hogan, M. Jenkin, S. Goldsworthy, L. Rose, and A. Dubrowski. Interprofessional care simulator for critical care education. In *Proceedings of the 2008 Conference on Future Play: Research, Play, Share*, Future Play '08, pages 260–261, New York, NY, USA, 2008. ACM. ISBN 978-1-60558-218-4. doi: 10.1145/1496984.1497043.

[63] A Raij, A Kotranza, D.S. Lind, and Benjamin Lok. Virtual experiences for social perspective-taking. In *Virtual Reality Conference,*

2009. VR 2009. IEEE, pages 99–102, March 2009. doi: 10.1109/VR.
2009.4811005.

[64] J. Goncalves, T. M. Caracena, V. Equeira, and E. V. Vidal. Virtual
reality based system for nuclear safeguards applications. In *IAEA Symposium on International Safeguards 2010*, JRC61732, 2010.

[65] METI. Meti, 2014. URL http://www.meti.com/.

[66] MSEC.   Msec,   2014.   URL   http://www.
medical-supplies-equipmentcompany.com.

[67] SimMan. Simman, 2014. URL http://www.laerdal.com/doc/86/
SimMan.

[68] F. Semeraro, A. Frisoli, M. Bergamasco, and E. L. Cerchiari. Virtual reality enhanced mannequin (vrem) that is well received by resuscitation
experts. *Resuscitation*, 80(4):489–492, April 2009. ISSN 0300-9572.
doi: 10.1016/j.resuscitation.2008.12.016.

[69] A.S. Carlin, H. G. Hoffman, and S. Weghorst. Virtual reality and tactile augmentation in the treatment of spider phobia: a case report. *Behaviour Research and Therapy*, 35(2):153 – 158, 1997. ISSN 0005-
7967. doi: http://dx.doi.org/10.1016/S0005-7967(96)00085-X.

[70] J. Gershon, P. Anderson, K. Graap, E. Zimand, L. Hodges, and B.O.
Rothbaum. Virtual reality exposure therapy in the treatment of anxiety
disorders. *Sci Rev Ment Health Pract*, 1:76–81, 2000.

[71] E. Zimand, P. Anderson, J. Gershon, K. Graap, L. Hodges, and B.O.
Rothbaum. Virtual reality therapy: innovative treatment for anxiety
disorders. *Prim Psychiatry*, 9:51–54, 2002.

[72] C. Culbertson, S. Nicolas, I. Zaharovits, E. D. London, R. II
De La Garza, A. L. Brody, and T. F. Newton. Methamphetamine
craving induced in an online virtual reality environment. *Pharma-
col Biochem Behav*, 96(4):454–460, 2010. doi: 10.1016/j.pbb.2010.
07.005.

[73] C. Perpina, C. Botella, and R.M. Banos. Virtual reality in eating disorders. *European Eating Disorders Review*, 11:261–278, 2003.

[74] G. Riva. The key to unlocking the virtual body: Virtual reality in the
treatment of obesity and eating disorders. *Journal of Diabetes Science
and Technology*, 5:283–292, 2011.

[75] H. Hoffman. Snowy virtual environments help by burning injuries,
2008. URL https://www.youtube.com/watch?v=jNIqyyypojg.
University of Washington, Seattle, WA.

[76] H. Hoffman. Virtual reality therapy effective in reducing burn patients in pain, 2009. University of Washington, Seattle, WA. Online article writen by Michelle Minkoff.

[77] J.I. Gold, S.H. Kim, A.J. Kant, M.H. Joseph, and A.S. Rizzo. Effectiveness of virtual reality for pediatric pain distraction during i.v. placement. *Cyberpsychol Behav*, 9(2):207–212, 2006.

[78] J-M. Normand, E. Giannopoulos, B. Spanlang, and M. Slater. Multisensory stimulation can induce an illusion of larger belly size in immersive virtual reality. *PLoS ONE*, 6:e16128, 2011.

[79] K. Kilteni, J.-M. Normand, M. V. Sanchez-Vives, and M. Slater. Extending body space in immersive virtual reality: A very long arm illusion. *PLoS ONE*, 7(7):e40867, 2012.

[80] V. I. Petkova and H. H. Ehrsson. If i were you: Perceptual illusion of body swapping. *PLoS ONE*, 3(12):e3832. doi:10.1371/journal.pone.0003832, 2008.

[81] C. Preston and H. H. Ehrsson. Illusory changes in body size modulate body satisfaction in a way that is related to non-clinical eating disorder psychopathology. *PLoS ONE*, 9(1):e85773, 01 2014.

[82] I. H.S. Mischner, H. T. van Schie, D. H.J. Wigboldus, R. B. van Baaren, and R. C.M.E. Engels. Thinking big: The effect of sexually objectifying music videos on bodily self-perception in young women. *Body Image*, 10(1):26 – 34, 2013.

[83] B.E. Riecke, P. A. Behbahani, and C. D. Shaw. Display size does not affect egocentric distance perception of naturalistic stimuli. In *Proceedings of the ACM SIGGRAPH Symposium on Applied Perception in Graphics and Visualization*, APGV 2009, pages 15–18, New York, NY, USA, 2009. ACM.

[84] Oculus VR. Oculus rift, 2014. URL http://www.oculusvr.com/.

[85] C. Charbonnier, N. Magnenat-Thalmann, C.D. Becker, P. Hoffmeyer, and J. Menetrey. An integrated platform for hip joint osteoarthritis analysis: Design, implementation and results. *Int J CARS*, 351-358, April 2010.

[86] André Miede. Latex templates: Classicthesis typographic thesis, 2014. URL http://www.latextemplates.com/template/classicthesis-typographic-thesis.

[87] Rocketbox Studios GmbH. Complete characters library hd, 2014. URL http://www.rocketbox.de/.

[88] Tübingen Perceiving Systems, Max Planck Institute for Intelligent Systems. 3d models generated from 3d scans, 2014. URL http://ps.is.tuebingen.mpg.de/.

[89] M. Mori. Bukimi no tani the uncanny valley (originally in japanese, translated by karl f. macdorman and takashi minato). *Energy*, 7(4): 33–35, 1970.

[90] J. Cassell. Embodied conversational agents: Representation and intelligence in user interface. *AI Magazine*, 22(3):67–83, 2001.

[91] R. McDonnell and M. Breidt. Face reality: Investigating the uncanny valley for virtual faces. In *ACM SIGGRAPH ASIA 2010 Sketches*, SA '10, pages 41:1–41:2, New York, NY, USA, 2010. ACM. ISBN 978-1-4503-0523-5. doi: 10.1145/1899950.1899991.

[92] S. Turkle. *Life on the Screen: Identity in the Age of the Internet*. Simon and Schuster Trade, 1995. ISBN 0684803534.

[93] R. A. Dunn and R. E. Guadagno. My avatar and me: Gender and personality predictors of avatar-self discrepancy. *Computers in Human Behavior*, 28(1):97 – 106, 2012. ISSN 0747-5632. doi: http://dx.doi.org/10.1016/j.chb.2011.08.015.

[94] Tübingen Perceiving Systems, Max Planck Institute for Intelligent Systems. Body visualizer, 2011. URL http://bodyvisualizer.com. MPI IS Perceiving Systems Department, Copyright Max Planck Gesellschaft. (July 2, 2014). Retrieved July 2, 2014 from : http://bodyvisualizer.com/.

[95] Microsoft. Microsoft kinect, 2014. URL http://www.microsoft.com/en-us/kinectforwindows/.

[96] A Bared, A Rashan, B Caughlin, and D Toriumi. Lower lateral cartilage repositioning: objective analysis using 3-dimensional imaging. *JAMA Facial Plast Surg*, 16(4):261–267, Jul-Aug 2014. doi: 10.1001/jamafacial.2013.2552.

[97] Y.-A. Lee, M. L. Damhorst, M.-S. Lee, J. M. Kozar, and P. Martin. Older women's clothing fit and style concerns and their attitudes toward the use of 3d body scanning. *Clothing and Textiles Research Journal*, 30:102–118, April 2012. doi: 10.1177/0887302X11429741.

[98] 3dMD Systems. 3dmd systems, 2014. URL http://www.3dmd.com/. 2014 3dMD - All Rights Reserved.

[99] Tübingen Perceiving Systems, Max Planck Institute for Intelligent Systems. 3d static scanner, 2014. URL http://ps.is.tuebingen.mpg.de/static_capture. MPI IS Perceiving Systems Department, Copyright 2012-2014 Max Planck Gesellschaft.

[100] Tübingen Perceiving Systems, Max Planck Institute for Intelligent Systems. 3d dynamic scanner, 2014. URL http://ps.is.tuebingen.mpg.de/dynamic_capture. MPI IS Perceiving Systems Department, Copyright 2012-2014 Max Planck Gesellschaft.

[101] Inc Leap Motion. Leap motion, 2014. URL https://www.leapmotion.com/. Copyright © 2014, Leap Motion, Inc.

[102] A. Shapiro, A. Feng, R. Wang, H. Li, G. Medioni, M. Bolas, and E. Suma. Fast avatar creation, 2014. Project collaboration between the USC ICT's Character Animation and Simulation Group from Ari Shapiro and Andrew Feng, USC ICT's Mixed Reality Lab with Evan Suma and Mark Bolas, and the USC Institute for Robotics and Intelligence Systems with Wang Ruizhe and Gerard Medioni with contributions from USC Viterbi's Hao Li.

[103] T. Weise, S. Bouaziz, H. Li, and M. Pauly. Realtime performance-based facial animation. *ACM Trans. Graph.*, 30(4):77:1–77:10, July 2011. ISSN 0730-0301. doi: 10.1145/2010324.1964972.

[104] J. K. Hodgins, S. Jürg, C O'Sullivan, S. I. Park, and M. Mahler. The saliency of anomalies in animated human characters. 2010.

[105] K. Dobs, I Bülthoff, M. Breidt, Q. C. Vuong, C. Curio, and J. Schultz. Quantifying human sensitivity to spatio-temporal information in dynamic faces. *Vision Research*, 100(0):78 – 87, 2014. ISSN 0042-6989. doi: http://dx.doi.org/10.1016/j.visres.2014.04.009.

[106] M Furniss. Motion capture, Dec. 1999. URL http://web.mit.edu/comm-forum/papers/furniss.html.

[107] Vicon. © vicon motion systems ltd. uk registered no. 1801446, 2014. URL http://www.vicon.com/.

[108] Xsens. Xsens mvn, 2014. URL http://www.xsens.com/products/xsens-mvn/. Copyright © 2014.

[109] D. Roetenberg, H. Luinge, and P. Slycke. Xsens MVN: Full 6DOF Human Motion Tracking Using Miniature Inertial Sensors. Technical report, xsens, 2009.

[110] Autodesk Inc. © 2014 autodesk inc, 2014. URL http://www.autodesk.com/.

[111] Blender Org. Blender, 2014. URL http://www.blender.org/.

[112] D. Hirshberg, M. Loper, E. Rachlin, and M.J. Black. Coregistration: Simultaneous alignment and modeling of articulated 3D shape. In A. Fitzgibbon et al. (Eds.), editor, *European Conf. on Computer Vision (ECCV)*, LNCS 7577, Part IV, pages 242–255. Springer-Verlag, October 2012.

[113] F. Bogo, J. Romero, M. Loper, and M. J. Black. FAUST: Dataset and evaluation for 3D mesh registration. In *Proceedings IEEE Conf. on Computer Vision and Pattern Recognition (CVPR)*, Columbus, Ohio, USA, June 2014.

[114] A. Weiss, D. Hirshberg, and M.J. Black. Home 3D body scans from noisy image and range data. In *International Conference on Computer Vision (ICCV)*, pages 1951–1958, Barcelona, November 2011. IEEE.

[115] E. Lantz. A survey of large-scale immersive displays. In *Proceedings of the 2007 Workshop on Emerging Displays Technologies: Images and Beyond: The Future of Displays and Interacton*, EDT '07, New York, NY, USA, 2007. ACM. ISBN 978-1-59593-669-1. doi: 10.1145/1278240.1278241.

[116] C. Cruz-Neira, D. J. Sandin, and T. A. DeFanti. Surround-screen projection-based virtual reality: the design and implementation of the cave. In *Proceedings of the 20th annual conference on Computer graphics and interactive techniques*, SIGGRAPH 1993, pages 135–142, New York, NY, USA, 1993. ACM.

[117] E. Lantz. Large-scale immersive displays in entertainment and education. In *2nd Annual Immersive Projection Technology Workshop*, May 11-12 1998.

[118] I. E. Sutherland. A head-mounted three dimensional display. In *Proceedings of the December 9-11, 1968, Fall Joint Computer Conference, Part I*, AFIPS '68 (Fall, part I), pages 757–764, New York, NY, USA, 1968. ACM. doi: 10.1145/1476589.1476686.

[119] © 2013 Virtual Realities Ltd. nVisor sx60, 2013. URL http://www.vrealities.com/products/head-mounted-displays/nvisor-sx60.

[120] B. J. Mohler, H. H. Bülthoff, W. B. Thompson, and S. H. Creem-Regehr. A Full-Body Avatar Improves Distance Judgments in Virtual Environments. In *Proceedings of the ACM SIGGRAPH Symposium on Applied Perception in Graphics and Visualization*, APGV 2008, pages 194–197, New York, NY, USA, 2008. ACM.

[121] B. Williams, T. Rasor, and G. Narasimham. Distance perception in virtual environments: a closer look at the horizon and the error. In *Proceedings of the ACM SIGGRAPH Symposium on Applied Perception in Graphics and Visualization*, APGV 2009, pages 7–10, New York, NY, USA, 2009. ACM.

[122] P. Willemsen, A. A. Gooch, W. B. Thompson, and S. H. Creem-Regehr. Effects of stereo viewing conditions on distance perception in virtual environments. *Presence: Teleoperators and Virtual Environments*, 17 (1):91 – 101, 2008.

[123] © 2013 · Virtual Realities Ltd. nVisor sx111, 2013. URL http://www.vrealities.com/products/head-mounted-displays/nvisor-sx111.

[124] K. Kilteni, I Bergstom, and M. Slater. Drumming in immersive virtual reality: The body shapes the way we play. In *Virtual Reality (VR), 2013 IEEE*, pages 1–1, March 2013.

[125] M. Mine and A. Yoganandan. Building (disney) castles in the air. ISIS3D, 2013. ACM.

[126] W. B. Thompson. *In Fundamentals of Computer Graphics (Second): Visual perception*. Ed. A. K. Peters, Ltd., Natick, MA, USA,, 2005.

[127] D. Vishwanath, A. R. Girshick, and M. S. Banks. Why pictures look right when viewed from the wrong place. *Nat Neurosci*, 8(19):2457 – 2473, 2005.

[128] M. S. Banks, H. F. Rose, D. Vishwanath, and A. R. Girshick. Where should you sit to watch a movie? *SPIE*, 5666:316–325, 2005.

[129] M. S. Banks, R. T. Held, and A. R. Girshick. Perception of 3-d layout in stereo displays. *Inf Disp (1975)*, 25(1):12–16, 2009.

[130] Eyevis. Visual solutions, 2014. URL http://eyevis.de.

[131] C. Masone, P. Giordano, and H. H. Bülthoff. Mechanical design and control of the new 7-dof cybermotion simulator. In *IEEE International Conference on Robotics and Automation*, ICRA 2011, pages 4935–4942, Piscataway, NJ, USA, 2011. IEEE.

[132] P. Willemsen, A. A. Gooch, W. B. Thompson, and S. H. Creem-Regehr. Effects of stereo viewing conditions on distance perception in virtual environments. *Presence: Teleoperators & Virtual Environments*, 17(1): 91–101, 2008.

[133] C. A. Encyclopedia Britannica, Primary Contributor: Villee. Body morphology, 2014. URL http://www.britannica.com/EBchecked/topic/392797/morphology.

[134] F. de Vignemont. Embodiment, ownership and disownership. *Consciousness and Cognition*, 20:81–93, 2011.

[135] P. Schilder. *The Image and Appearance of the Human Body: Studies in the Constructive Energies of the Psyche*. New York: International University Press, 1935.

[136] G. Riva. Neuroscience and eating disorders: The role of the medial temporal lobe. *Nature Precedings*, page 2, 2010.

[137] T. Hashimoto and A. Iriki. Dissociations between the horizontal and dorsoventral axes in body-size perception. *Eur J Neurosci*, 37(11): 1747–1753, 2013.

[138] M. R. Longo and P. Haggard. Implicit body representations and the conscious body image. *Acta Psychologica*, 141(2):164 – 168, 2012.

[139] M. Tsakiris, G. Prabhu, and P. Haggard. Having a body versus moving your body: How agency structures body-ownership. *Consciousness and Cognition*, 15(2):423–432, 2006.

[140] M. Botvinick and J. Cohen. Rubber hands 'feel' touch that eyes see. *Nature*, 391:756, 1998.

[141] M. Tsakiris and P. Haggard. The rubber hand illusion revisited: Visuo-tactile integration and self-attribution. *Journal of Experimental Psychology: Human Perception and Performance*, 31(1):80–91, 2005.

[142] M. R. Longo and P. Haggard. What is it like to have a body? *Current Directions in Psychological Science*, 21(2):140–145, 2012.

[143] M. R. Longo, F. Schuur, M. P. M. Kammers, M. Tsakiris, and P. Haggard. What is embodiment? a psychometric approach. *Cognition*, 107: 978–998, 2008.

[144] M. R. Longo and P Haggard. Sense of agency primes manual motor responses. *Perception*, 38(1):69–78, 2009.

[145] V. I. Petkova, M. Bjarnsdotter, G. Gentile, T. Jonsson, T-Q. Li, and H.H. Ehrsson. From part- to whole-body ownership in the multisensory brain. *Current Biology*, 21(13):1118 – 1122, 2011. ISSN 0960-9822. doi: http://dx.doi.org/10.1016/j.cub.2011.05.022.

[146] R. Newport, R. Pearce, and C. Preston. Fake hands in action: embodiment and control of supernumerary limbs. *Experimental Brain Research*, 204(3):385–395, 2010.

[147] A. Kalckert and H. H. Ehrsson. Moving a rubber hand that feels like your own: A dissociation of ownership and agency. *Frontiers in Human Neuroscience*, 6:40–40, 2012.

[148] F. Pavani, C. Spence, and J. Driver. Visual capture of touch: Out-of-the-body experiences with rubber gloves. *Psychological Science*, 11: 353–359, 2000.

[149] M. Slater, B. Spanlang, M. V. Sanchez-Vives, and O. Blanke. First person experience of body transfer in virtual reality. *PLoS ONE*, 5(5): e10564, 05 2010.

[150] M. R. Longo, S. Cardozo, and P. V. Haggard. Visual enhancement of touch and the body self. *Consciousness and Cognition*, 17:1181–1191, 2008.

[151] B. van der Hoort, A. Guterstam, and H. H. Ehrsson. Being barbie: The size of one's own body determines the perceived size of the world. *PLoS ONE*, 6(5):e20195, 2011.

[152] B. Lenggenhager, T. Tadi, T. Metzinger, and O. Blanke. Video ergo sum: Manipulating bodily self-consciousness. *Science*, 317(5841): 1096 – 1099, 2007.

[153] D. Perez-Marcos, M. Slater, and M. V. Sanchez-Vives. Inducing a virtual hand ownership illusion through a brain-computer interface. *NeuroReport*, 20:589–594, 2009.

[154] M. Slater, D. Perez-Marcos, H. H. Ehrsson, and M. V. Sanchez-Vives. Inducing illusory ownership of a virtual body. *Frontiers in Neuroscience*, 3:214–220, 2009.

[155] V. I. Petkova, M. Khoshnevis, and H. H. Ehrsson. The perspective matters! multisensory integration in ego-centric reference frames determines full body ownership. *Frontiers in Psychology*, 2(35), 2011.

[156] D. Banakou, R. Groten, and M. Slater. Illusory ownership of a virtual child body causes overestimation of object sizes and implicit attitude changes. *Proceedings of the National Academy of Sciences*, 110(31): 12846–12851, 2013. doi: 10.1073/pnas.1306779110.

[157] J. J. Gibson. *The Ecological Approach to Visual Perception*. Houghton Mifflin, 1979.

[158] J. K. Witt, D. R. Proffitt, and W. Epstein. Tool use affects perceived distance, but only when you intend to use it. *Journal of Experimental Psychology: Human Perception and Performance*, 31:880–888, 2005.

[159] J. K. Stefanucci and M. N. Geuss. Big people, little world:the body influences size perception. *Perception*, 38:1782 – 1795, 2009.

[160] W. H. Warren and S. Whang. Visual guidance of walking through apertures: body-scaled information for affordances. *Journal of Experimental Psychology: Human Perception and Performance*, 13:371 – 383, 1987.

[161] C. F. Michaels. Affordances: Four points of debate. *Ecological Psychology*, 15:135–148, 2003.

[162] A. Fallon and P. Rozin. Sex differences in perceptions of desirable body shape. *Journal of Abnormal Psychology*, 94(1):102–105, 1985.

[163] A.J. Stunckard, T. Sorensen, and F. Schulsinger. *The genetics of neurological and psychiatric disorders*. Raven Press: New York, 1983.

[164] F. Askevold. Measuring body image: Preliminary report on a new method. *Psychotherapy and Psychosomatics*, 26:71–77, 1975.

[165] P. D. Slade and G. F. Russell. Awareness of body dimensions in anorexia nervosa: Cross-sectional and longitudinal studies. *Psychological Medicine*, 3:188–199, 1973.

[166] C. Farrell, M. Lee, and R. Shafran. Assessment of body size estimation: a review. *European Eating Disorders Review*, 13(2):75–88, 2005.

[167] T. F. Cash, D. W. Cash, and J. W. Butters. Mirror, mirror, on the wall: Contrast effects and self-evaluations of physical attractiveness. *Personality and Social Psychology Bulletin*, 9(3):351–358, 1983.

[168] C. T. Fuentes, M. R. Longo, and Haggard P. Body image distortions in healthy adults. *Acta Psychologica*, 144(2):344 – 351, 2013. ISSN 0001-6918. doi: http://dx.doi.org/10.1016/j.actpsy.2013.06.012.

[169] T. F. Cash and E.A. Deagle. The nature and extent of body-image disturbances in anorexia nervosa and bulimia nervosa: a meta-analysis. *The International journal of eating disorders*, 22:107–25, 1997.

[170] M. L. Glucksman and J. Hirsch. The response of obese patients to weight reduction: A clinical evaluation of behavior. *Psychosomatic Medicine*, 30:1–11, 1968.

[171] M.A.M. Smeets, F. Smit, G.E.M. Panhuysen, and J.D. Ingleby. The influence of methodological differenceson the outcome of body size estimation studies in anorexia nervosa. *British Journal of Clinical Psychology*, 36:263–277, 1997.

[172] R. E. McCabe, T. McFarlane, J. Polivy, and M. P. Olmsted. Eating disorders, dieting, and the accuracy of self-reported weight. *International Journal of Eating Disorders*, 29(1):59–64, 2001.

[173] J. Doolen, P. T. Alpert, and S. K. Miller. Parental disconnect between perceived and actual weight status of children: A metasynthesis of the current research. *Journal of the American Academy of Nurse Practitioners*, 21(3):160–166, 2009. ISSN 1745-7599.

[174] G. Riva. Neuroscience and eating disorders: The role of the medial temporal lobe. *Available from Nature Precedings <http://hdl.handle.net/10101/npre.2010.4235.1>*, 2010.

[175] R. J. Freeman, C. D. Thomas, L. Solyom, and M. A. Hunter. A modified video camera for measuring body image distortion: Technical description and reliability. *Psychological Medicine*, 14:411–416, 1984.

[176] D. A. Brodie, P. D. Slade, and H. Rose. Reliability measures in distorting body-image. *Perceptual and Motor Skills*, 69:723–732, 1989.

[177] A.C. Traub and J.J. Orbach. Psychophysical studies of body-image: I. the adjustable body-distorting mirror. *Archives of General Psychiatry*, 11(1):53–66, 1964.

[178] A. J. Schofield, P. Sun, and G. Mazzilli. *Shape Perception in Human and Computer Vision: An Interdisciplinary Perspective*. Springer-Verlag London, 2013.

[179] R.W. Fleming, A. Torralba, and Adelson E.H. Specular reflections and the perception of shape. *J. Vis.*, 4(9):798–820, 2004.

[180] P. Thompson and K. Mikellidou. Applying the helmholtz illusion to fashion: horizontal stripes wonât make you look fatter. *i-Perception*, 2 (1):69–76, 2011.

[181] J. Loomis, Y. Lippa, R. L. Klatzky, and R. G. Golledge. Spatial updating of locations specified by 3-d sound and spatial language. *Journal of Experimental Psychology: Learning, Memory, and Cognition*, 28(2): 335–345, 2002.

[182] S. A. Kuhl, S. H. Creem-Regehr, and W. B. Thompson. Individual differences in accuracy of blind walking to targets on the floor. *Journal of Vision*, 6(6):726, 2006.

[183] B. R. Kunz, L. Wouters, D. Smith, W. B. Thompson, and S. H. Creem-Regehr. Revisiting the effect of quality of graphics on distance judgments in virtual environments: A comparison of verbal reports and blind walking. *Attention, Perception, and Psychophysics*, 71(6):1284–1293, 2009.

[184] B. Thompson, P. Willemsen, A. A. Gooch, S. H. Creem-Regehr, J. M. Loomis, and A. C. Beall. Does the quality of the computer graphics matter when judging distances in visually immersive environments? *Presence: Teleoperators and Virtual Environments*, 13(5):560–571, 2004.

[185] B. J. Mohler. *The effect of feedback within a virtual environment on human distance perception and adaptation.* PhD thesis, University of Utah, Salt Lake City, UT, USA, 2007.

[186] A. R. Richardson and D. Waller. The effect of feedback training on distance estimation in virtual environments. *Applied Cognitive Psychology*, 19(8):1089–1108, 2005.

[187] E. J. Gibson. The effect of prior training with a scale of distance on absolute and relative judgments of distance over ground. *Journal of Experimental Psychology*, 50(2):997–1005, 1955.

[188] J. K. Witt, J. K. Stefanucci, C. R. Riener, and D. R. Proffitt. Seeing beyond the target: environmental context affects distance perception. *Perception*, 36(12):1752–1768, 2007.

[189] S. A. Kuhl, W. B. Thompson, and S. H. Creem-Regehr. Hmd calibration and its effects on distance judgments. *ACM Transactions on Applied Perception*, 6(3):1–20, 2009. ISSN 15443558. doi: 10.1145/1577755.1577762.

[190] M. Leyrer, S.A. Linkenauger, H.H. Bülthoff, and B. J. Mohler. Eye height manipulations: A possible solution to counter underestimation

of egocentric distances in head-mounted displays. *ACM Trans. Appl. Percept.*, 12(1):1:1–1:23, February 2015. ISSN 1544-3558. doi: 10.1145/2699254. URL http://doi.acm.org/10.1145/2699254.

[191] I. P. Howard. *Seeing in depth*, volume 2. I. Porteous, 2002.

[192] E. J. Gibson, J. J. Gibson, O. W. Smith, and H. Flock. Motion parallax as a determinant of perceived depth. *Journal of Experimental Psychology*, 58(1):40–51, 1959.

[193] L. Leroy, P. Fuchs, and G. Moreau. Some experiments about shape perception in stereoscopic displays. 7237:1–11, jan 2009.

[194] A. C. Beall, J. M. Loomis, J. W. Philbeck, and T. G. Fikes. Absolute motion parallax weakly determines visual scale in real and virtual environments. In *Human Vision, Visual Processing, and Digital Displays*, HVVPDD 1995, pages 288–297, 1995.

[195] S. J. Watt, K. Akeley, M. O. Ernst, and M. S. Banks. Focus cues affect perceived depth. *Journal of Vision*, 5(10):834–862, 2005.

[196] D. M. Hoffman, A. R. Girshick, K. Akeley, and M. S. Banks. Vergence-accommodation conflicts hinder visual performance and cause visual fatigue. *Journal of Vision*, 8(3):1–30, 2008.

[197] P.C. Treleaven. Sizing us up. *IEEE Spectrum*, 41:28–31, 2004.

[198] M. P. Reed. A pilot study of three-dimensional child anthropometry for vehicle safety analysis. *Proceedings of the Human Factors and Ergonomics Society Annual Meeting*, 56(1):2326–2330, 2012. doi: 10.1177/1071181312561489.

[199] P. Volino, N. Magnenat-Thalmann, and F. Faure. A simple approach to nonlinear tensile stiffness for accurate cloth simulation. *ACM Trans. Graph.*, 28(4):105:1–105:16, September 2009. ISSN 0730-0301. doi: 10.1145/1559755.1559762.

[200] J. E. Bos, W Bles, and E. L. Groen. A theory on visually induced motion sickness. *Displays*, 29(2):47 – 57, 2008.

[201] M. Di Luca. New method to measure end-to-end delay of virtual reality. *Presence: eleoperators and Virtual Environments*, 19(6):569–584, 2010.

[202] M. Geuss, J. Stefanucci, S. Creem-Regehr, and W. B. Thompson. Can I pass?: using affordances to measure perceived size in virtual environments. In *Proceedings of the 7th Symposium on Applied Perception in Graphics and Visualization*, APGV '10, pages 61–64, New York, NY, USA, 2010. ACM.

[203] M. Dobricki and S. de la Rosa. The structure of conscious bodily self-perception during full-body illusions. *PLoS ONE*, 8:e83840, 2013.

[204] M. Tsakiris, M. R. Longo, and P. Haggard. Having a body versus moving your body: Neural signatures of agency and body-ownership. *Neuropsychologia*, (48):2740–2749, 2010.

[205] I. V. Piryankova, S. de la Rosa, U. Kloos, H. H. Bülthoff, and B. J. Mohler. Egocentric distance perception in large screen immersive displays. *Displays*, 34(2):153 – 164, 2013. ISSN 0141-9382. doi: http://dx.doi.org/10.1016/j.displa.2013.01.001.

[206] I. V. Alexandrova, P. T. Teneva, S. de la Rosa, U. Kloos, H. H. Bülthoff, and B. J. Mohler. Egocentric distance judgments in a large screen display immersive virtual environment. In *Proceedings of the 7th Symposium on Applied Perception in Graphics and Visualization*, APGV 2010, pages 57–60, New York, NY, USA, 2010. ACM.

[207] V. Couture, M. S. Langer, and S. Roy. Analysis of disparity distortions in omnistereoscopic displays. *ACM Transactions on Applied Perception*, 7:25:1–25:13, July 2010.

[208] J. Knapp. *The Visual Perception of Egocentric Distance in Virtual Environments*. PhD thesis, University of California at Santa Barbara, Dec 1999.

[209] D. Anguelov, P. Srinivasan, D. Koller, S. Thrun, J. Rodgers, and J. Davis. SCAPE: Shape completion and animation of people. *ACM Transactions on Graphics (ToG)*, 24(3):408–416, 2005.

[210] K. M. Robinette and H. Daanen. The Caesar project: A 3-D surface anthropometry survey. In *Proc. of Second Int. Conference on 3- D Digital Imaging and Modeling*, pages 380–386, Ottawa, Canada, 1999.

[211] H. H. Bülthoff and S. Edelman. Psychophysical support for a two-dimensional view interpolation theory of object recognition. In *Proceedings of the National Academy Science of the United States of America*, 89(1), pages 60–64. Houghton Mifflin, 1992.

[212] C. Wallraven, A. Schwaninger, S. Schuhmacher, and H. H. Bülthoff. View-based recognition of faces in man and machine: Re-visiting inter-extra-ortho. In Heinrich H. Bülthoff, Christian Wallraven, Seong-Whan Lee, and Tomaso A. Poggio, editors, *Biologically Motivated Computer Vision*, volume 2525 of *Lecture Notes in Computer Science*, pages 651–660. Springer Berlin Heidelberg, 2002.

[213] M. Rosenberg. Society and the adolescent self-image. In *Princeton, NJ:Princeton University Press*, 1965.

[214] F. A. Wichmann and N. J. Hill. The psychometric function: I. fitting, sampling and goodness-of-fit. *Perception and Psychophysics*, 63(8): 1293–1313, 2001.

[215] A Stuart and J.K. Ord. *Kendall's Advanced Theory of Statistics(6th edition)*. London: Edward Arnold, 1994.

DECLARATION

Selbstständigkeitserklärung

Ich, Ivelina Vesselinova Piryankova (geb. Alexandrova), erkläre hiermit, dass ich die zur Promotion eingereichte Arbeit mit dem Titel: *The influence of a self-avatar on space and body perception in immersive virtual reality*, selbständig verfasst (soweit nicht anderweitig durch den Verweis auf zugrunde liegende Veröffentlichungen gekennzeichnet), nur die angegebenen Quellen und Hilfsmittel benutzt und wörtlich oder inhaltlich übernommene Stellen als solche gekennzeichnet habe. Ich erkläre, dass die Richtlinien zur Sicherung guter wissenschaftlicher Praxis der Universität Tübingen (Beschluss des Senats vom 25.5.2000) beachtet wurden. Teile dieser Arbeit wurden in der vorliegenden Form im Zuge wissenschaftlicher Publikationen veröffentlicht und enthalten zu einem gewissen Anteil Überlegungen und Formulierungen der entsprechend ausgewiesenen Ko-Autoren. Die zugrunde liegenden Publikationen mit einer Auflistung der beteiligten Autoren sind in der Einführung zitiert. Ich versichere an Eides statt, dass diese Angaben wahr sind und dass ich nichts verschwiegen habe. Mir ist bekannt, dass die falsche Abgabe einer Versicherung an Eides statt mit Freiheitsstrafe bis zu drei Jahren oder mit Geldstrafe bestraft wird. Diese Promotionsarbeit wurde in gleicher oder ähnlicher Form in keinem anderen Studiengang als Prüfungsleistung vorgelegt.

Tübingen, 2014

Ivelina Vesselinova Piryankova,
April 16, 2015